The Jossey-Bass Nonprofit Sector Series also includes:

The National Society of Fund Raising Executives

Since 1960 the National Society of Fund Raising Executives (NSFRE) has been the leading professional association for those who advance philanthropy through ethical fund raising. The association has more than 16,000 members in 141 chapters throughout the United States, Canada, and Mexico. Through its advocacy, research, education, and certification programs, NSFRE fosters the development and growth of fund-raising professionals, works to advance philanthropy and volunteerism, and promotes high ethical standards in fund raising.

NSFRE strives not only to prepare fund-raising professionals to meet the increasing demands placed on philanthropy and the not-for-profit sector but also to educate the public about the important role of philanthropy and volunteerism. To this end, NSFRE:

• Promotes consistent, high standards of professional practice to ensure donor trust and guard against abuses that can occur in the fund-raising process.
• Requires members to comply with a Code of Ethical Principles and Standards of Professional Practice (Code), which is designed to provide concrete guidelines for fund-raising professionals in philanthropic organizations. The code is underscored with an enforcement policy, which is governed by the NSFRE Ethics Committee.
• Was instrumental in creating the "Donor Bill of Rights," a document outlining what donors have the right to expect from the charitable organizations to which they contribute.
• Certifies fund-raising executives through the Certified Fund Raising Executive (CFRE) program and the Advanced Certified Fund Raising Executive (ACFRE) program. These credentials, held by more than 3,500 fund-raising professionals, verify experience and knowledge of fund raising.
• Provides education programs on fund raising. Programs include the annual International Conference on Fund Raising, the Executive Leadership Institute, the Fund Raising and the Law Conference, the Survey Course on Fund Raising, and the First Course in Fund Raising.
• Provides information about philanthropy through its Fund-Raising Resource Center, which houses a comprehensive collection of books, periodicals, speeches, and audiovisual materials on fund raising and the not-for-profit sector.
• Encourages research on fund raising and philanthropy.
• Supports legislation and regulations to encourage philanthropic giving and ethical fund raising.
• Publishes books to foster the development and growth of professional fund-raising executives.
• Disseminates a monthly syndicated column to educate citizens about fund raising and the not-for-profit sector.
• Publishes a quarterly journal, *Advancing Philanthropy*, which features current issues in philanthropy.

For additional information about NSFRE and its programs, please contact the organization at National Society of Fund Raising Executives, 1101 King Street, Suite 700, Alexandria, VA 22314–2967, (800) 666-FUND, (703) 684–0410, (703) 684–0540 (fax), nsfre@nsfre.org (e-mail).

A Note from the President

Who are we, those of us who commit our professional lives to the process of developing donors? Why do we spend our days and weeks and years toiling in the trenches, fund raising? What are the rewards of this exhilarating, demanding, and challenging career?

Until the research for this book was undertaken, we had no solid answers to these questions. Some might ask why the questions—and their answers—are important. My response is that we—those who help raise the philanthropic dollars that make *the* difference in a society—must know who we are and why we do what we do if we are to consider our work more than a career or a field of endeavor.

This book will help to strengthen professionalism in fund raising.

Research about a field of endeavor, its activities, and those who work within it is necessary if that field is to be considered a profession. The National Society of Fund Raising Executives (NSFRE) has incorporated into its mission statement language about the vital role that research plays in advancing philanthropy through education, training, and advocacy. Through its Research Council, the Society helps support research on the many dimensions of the philanthropic process.

Margaret Duronio's three-year research project on fund-raising professionals puts to rest some myths about us fund raisers and elicits information about what motivates us. Writing with fund-raising practitioner Eugene Tempel, she reveals that although we are diverse in many ways, we are bound together by commitment. If you are a fund-raising practitioner, you will learn much more about yourself in this book. The authors have contributed significantly to the body of knowledge about fund raising.

NSFRE is pleased to have sponsored Dr. Duronio's research through its Research Council. We express our gratitude to the Lilly Endowment for providing the funding and to Dr. Tempel for his ongoing support of the project.

PATRICIA F. LEWIS, CFRE
President and CEO
National Society of Fund Raising Executives

Fund Raisers

Fund Raisers

Their Careers, Stories, Concerns, and Accomplishments

Margaret A. Duronio, Eugene R. Tempel

Jossey-Bass Publishers • San Francisco

Substantial discounts on bulk quantities of Jossey-Bass books are available to corporations, professional associations, and other organizations. For details and discount information, contact the special sales department at Jossey-Bass Inc., Publishers (415) 433–1740; Fax (800) 605–2665.

For sales outside the United States, please contact your local Simon & Schuster International Office.

 Manufactured in the United States of America on Lyons Falls Pathfinder Tradebook. This paper is acid-free and 100 percent totally chlorine-free.

Library of Congress Cataloging-in-Publication Data

Duronio, Margaret A., date.
    Fund raisers : their careers, stories, concerns, and
accomplishments / Margaret A. Duronio, Eugene R. Tempel.
        p. cm. — (The Jossey-Bass nonprofit sector series)
    Includes bibliographical references and index.
    ISBN 0–7879–0307–8
    1. Fund raisers (Persons)—United States. 2. Fund raising—United
States. 3. Occupational surveys—United States. I. Tempel, Eugene
R., date. II. Title. III. Series.
HV41.9.U5D87 1997
363.7′0681—dc20   96–34626

FIRST EDITION
HB Printing   10 9 8 7 6 5 4 3 2 1
PB Printing   10 9 8 7 6 5 4 3 2 1

The Jossey-Bass Nonprofit Sector Series

Contents

List of Tables

Foreword

Who are fund raisers? How were they educated in fund-raising practice? What are their concerns? What motivates them? These are some of the questions addressed in this study. Fund raisers today debate whether fund raising is a profession or a field. That debate cannot continue without a better understanding of the people who practice fund raising. To address these and other questions, the National Society of Fund Raising Executives and the Indiana University Center on Philanthropy collaborated on a study conducted by Margaret A. Duronio and codirected by Eugene R. Tempel.

The authors have analyzed the results of the study and provide here a valuable overview of America's fund raisers.

This research establishes a baseline of information about fund raisers, how they came into the field, how they are progressing in their careers, what their values are, the issues that affect their work, how they view themselves and other fund raisers, and many other valuable insights. These insights are extraordinarily important because fund raisers are on the front line of organizations and have within their power the ability to build or destroy the public trust in charities.

The study is based on a mail survey, with returns from more than 1,700 individuals, and 82 in-depth interviews with fund raisers on their careers, their education, and their opinions about the issues and future of fund raising as a profession. Most of the fund raisers surveyed were members of professional associations. The authors estimate that only about half of all fund raisers are members of such associations; very little is known about the other half of the population. Characterizing this group of fund raisers remains a challenge for the field and is one of the recommendations the authors make for future research.

The paid fund-raising professional is very much a product of the early twentieth century, when large national charitable organizations were organized. Before that, fund raising was a calling among volunteers. During the twentieth century, continuous efforts to raise money for large efforts—such as the eradication of tuberculosis, heart disease, and cancer; building the endowments of colleges and universities; and supporting hospitals—have led to staffed fund-raising efforts. According to the authors, there may be as many as 50,000 paid fund raisers in this country today. Of those studied, most are well educated, have high ethical standards, and are committed to the missions of their organizations. A majority of fund raisers report that they have learned their skills from on-the-job experience, and most do not recommend formal education as the best way to learn about fund raising. Slightly more than half are women, and less than 5 percent are from minority groups. Most are paid fairly modest salaries; only a small percentage make over $100,000 annually.

The authors conclude that fund raising may never become a "true profession" but that it might adopt professional standards. The distinctions they draw here are worthwhile. Yet, even if fund raising is a field rather than a profession, the authors are concerned about the lack of education in philanthropy and its traditions, a deficiency seen at the general as well as professional levels, even in management programs. They believe that while association-based education programs are important, such programs do not redress the lack of teaching of the philanthropic tradition in undergraduate courses or in graduate programs of education, social science, the history of science, and other areas. Moving the development of the field forward will be difficult if such education is not readily available.

The authors also address issues that should be of great interest and concern to leaders of charitable organizations. One issue is the position of fund raising within organizations. A significant percentage of fund raisers reported that their programs are not part of the organization's planning. A high percentage of fund raisers are concerned about their public image, which they believe is low, especially as a result of recent scandals in organizations such as the United Way of America. Fund raisers understand that if public trust declines, their work becomes much more difficult. There is not enough effort to demonstrate to the public that most fund raisers are committed to their institutions and their causes. Most fund raisers in this study exhibited strong values and ethical commitments to their work; however, it is not clear that such values are understood even by the institutions for which these people work. A significant portion of fund raisers revealed that they did not like to ask for money. Some feel frustrated when their colleagues do not even want to discuss this discomfort.

This book provides an illuminating analysis of these and other issues as well as a profile of fund raisers. Those who are concerned about this occupation as part of a field or a profession can begin to come to terms with the challenges that lie ahead. One of the authors' recommendations for the future is to build a similar study on a longitudinal basis. But even more important, this volume lays out the elements from which organizational leaders and fund-raising professionals can build a blueprint for the future. At a time when government funding at all levels is declining, organizational leaders should be very supportive of the education of fund raisers, of their ethics and values as professionals, of their efforts to build public trust, and of their need to become more comfortable with the very important task of asking for money.

Thanks should go to the authors for a seminal piece of work. I hope that this volume and its findings receive the attention they deserve both from fund raisers and organizational leaders. The future of the field—and the future of many organizations—will depend on how well they use such findings.

July 1996

VIRGINIA HODGKINSON
Vice President, Research
INDEPENDENT SECTOR

Preface

In 1988, Virginia Hodgkinson, vice president for research at Independent Sector, who was serving as a member of the Research Committee of the National Society of Fund Raising Executives (NSFRE) Foundation, suggested that if fund raisers wished to be taken seriously as professionals, they needed to know much more about themselves. The Research Committee decided to champion such a study and collaborated with the Indiana University Center on Philanthropy to organize the study and secure funding. Eugene Tempel, vice chancellor for external affairs at Indiana University-Purdue University Indianapolis, and chair of the NSFRE Research Council, convened an advisory group to help design the study. Jeanne Harrah-Conforth, through the Indiana University Center on Philanthropy, organized the initial design and proposal for funding. The Lilly Endowment, Inc., and an anonymous donor provided the $220,000 grant for the study to the NSFRE, which worked with the Center on Philanthropy for conduct of the study. Gene Tempel and Dwight Burlingame, director of academic programs and research at the Center on Philanthropy, asked Peg Duronio to serve as codirector of the project with them and as principal investigator of the research.

We wrote this book to share the results of this research with fund raisers, researchers, and others interested in fund raising, philanthropy, and nonprofit organizations. The overarching purpose of the research was to support the systematic development of a base of knowledge about the people in the fund-raising field. The research is purely descriptive; we make no claims that this effort proves anything. However, we are fully confident that this research provides a comprehensive picture of the most important and most challenging issues facing fund raisers. We are equally confident that this research provides a strong foundation for further development of knowledge about fund raisers by identifying both numerous areas for additional research and by offering some direction about how that research might be framed. In addition, the research:

- Presents a comprehensive, detailed picture of contemporary fund raisers at all levels of professional achievement, working for and on behalf of the entire range of nonprofit organizations.
- Describes fund-raising practitioners, their education and other work experiences, and the issues they face in their work.
- Explores what motivates fund raisers and how they find rewards and satisfaction in their work.
- Identifies the trends and environmental conditions that currently influence fund raisers in their work.

Research Methodology and Overall Response

This research, a project conducted over a period of three years, involved two phases: a comprehensive mail survey followed by intensive personal interviews with selected survey respondents and a number of leaders in the fund-raising field. The mail survey was designed to collect information on demographic characteristics, career histories, career commitments and plans, and attitudes regarding the fund-raising field. We sent the survey to a stratified random sample of 2,501 members of the major professional organizations representing fund raisers: the Association for Healthcare Philanthropy (AHP), the Council for Advancement and Support of Education (CASE), and the National Society of Fund Raising Executives (NSFRE). The sample was designed to reflect the proportion of fund raisers working in each nonprofit subsector.

After three mailings, we received 1,748 responses. In the first two mailings, we sent two copies (one blue, one green) of the survey and asked recipients to complete the blue copy and to give the green copy to a colleague in fund raising who was not a member of one of the professional organizations in the direct mailing. We used this approach in an attempt to reach a broader range of practitioners than the membership lists could identify. It is estimated that of the approximately fifty thousand fund raisers at work in the United states today, perhaps less than 50 percent are accessible through membership lists of major professional organizations. It seems reasonable to assume that persons working in fund raising at smaller, less affluent organizations are less likely to be members of professional groups, because those organizations are less likely to be able either to cover membership fees for the staff or to provide salaries that allow staff to pay membership fees comfortably on their own. A thorough and accurate picture of the field would have to include fund raisers who are not members of professional associations. Unfortunately, our effort to reach this extended population was not very successful, netting only 326 returns from persons who received copies of the surveys from colleagues instead of directly from us. Additionally, responses on many of these surveys led us to believe that they were actually from people who were members of professional organizations.

For this reason, we combined all 1,748 responses and did not attempt to compare responses on blue forms (members) with responses on green forms (presumably nonmembers). The consistency of our findings with those of previous studies by professional organizations gives us confidence that our respondent sample accurately reflects fund raisers who are members of professional organizations. We are also confident that our respondents represent fund raisers working in specific kinds of nonprofit organizations in the same proportion they are estimated to occur in real life. However, since the large population of fund raisers who are not members remains unavailable for study, the major limitation of this study is that its findings can be generalized with confidence only to fund raisers who are members of professional organizations.

The interviews with eighty-two survey respondents were designed to complement survey responses, to explore career histories and career motivations in depth, and to compile information regarding interviewees' attitudes and values related to their work. The interviews covered four general areas: family background, education and career history, present position, and issues in fund raising. To stay within budget and time constraints, we selected nine areas across the country: Massachusetts and Connecticut; New York City; Western Pennsylvania; Washington, D.C. area; North and South Carolina and Georgia; Illinois; Wisconsin and Michigan; Houston area; and Southern California. Interviewees, who were survey respondents in these geographical areas, worked in large and small cities, suburbs, and rural areas, and in organizations with national reputations and with local or regional influence.

Overview of Chapters

Chapters One through Eight open with a section called Snapshots. These sections are descriptions of some of the eighty-two people interviewed for this research. The snapshots are intended to provide examples of fund raisers whose career experiences illustrate the issues under consideration. After the Snapshots section, Chapter One presents the critical issues facing the fund-raising field and the nonprofit environment that forms the background for the work of fund raising. Chapters Two through Eight present the qualitative and quantitative data from the research. Chapter Two describes typical fund raisers and demographic characteristics of survey respondents, such as educational background and titles at work. Chapters Three and Four describe career histories in fund raising, including years in the fund-raising field, previous career experiences, and some factors involved in career decisions. Chapter Five is devoted to a discussion of compensation in fund raising. Chapter Six addresses several related issues including learning about fund raising, improving the practice of fund raising, and ethical aspects of fund raising. In Chapter Seven, we report on respondents' opinions about the personal characteristics, skills, and areas of professional knowledge of those they regard as the best fund raisers in the field. In Chapter Eight, drawing from all the data provided by the research, we return to the list of critical issues first presented in Chapter One and discuss these issues in some detail. Chapter Nine presents our conclusions and recommendations for practice for fund raisers, nonprofit organizations, and fund-raising professional organizations, as well as for further research.

Acknowledgments

We want to acknowledge with gratitude the support and assistance of colleagues and research assistants in our respective offices who took on additional responsibilities so that we could work on this manuscript. Peg Duronio extends particularly heartfelt thanks to Sue Steele at the University of Pittsburgh, who ran interference, put in hours and hours of overtime, and took on numerous challenges so this book could be finished. We both want to acknowledge with deep appreciation our spouses, Bill Wilson and Mary Tempel, whose support made—and continues to make—all the difference.

April 1996

MARGARET A. DURONIO
Pittsburgh, Pennsylvania

EUGENE R. TEMPEL
Indianapolis, Indiana

The Authors

Margaret A. Duronio is director of planning and administration for the office of the vice chancellor for institutional advancement at the University of Pittsburgh. She earned a B.A. degree (1969) in English at Pennsylvania State University and a master's degree in social work (1971) and doctoral degree (1985) in education (higher education and research methodology) at the University of Pittsburgh. Before joining the staff at Pitt, she worked as an internal management consultant in a health care system and as a marital therapist in a social service agency. As project director and principal investigator of five national studies on fund raising, Duronio has published one book and numerous articles and papers.

Eugene R. Tempel is vice chancellor for external affairs at Indiana University-Purdue University Indianapolis, where he also serves part-time as executive director of The Fund Raising School, and is associate professor of philanthropic studies at the Indiana University Center on Philanthropy. He earned a B.A. degree (1970) in English and philosophy at St. Benedict College and a master's degree (1974) in English and Ed.D. degree (1985) in higher education administration at Indiana University, Bloomington. As one of the founders of the Indiana University Center on Philanthropy, Tempel has been a proponent of the development of knowledge about fund raising and is particularly concerned about the ethics of fund raising and the relationship between fund raising and philanthropy. Tempel has authored several articles and chapters on fund raising and has served as vice chair of the National Society of Fund Raising Executives. He is a past chair of the NSFRE Foundation and of the NSFRE Research Council and serves on the boards of several nonprofit organizations.

Chapter One

Challenges and Opportunities in Fund Raising

As we use the term, *fund raisers* refers to people whose jobs involve the acquisition of revenues from private sources for nonprofit organizations. Some of those people, as we will indicate in later chapters, object to that term and also object to use of the term *fund raising* to describe what they do. In spite of these objections and our awareness of them, we have persisted in this usage for two reasons. The first is strictly pragmatic: this is the simplest way to describe the people and the occupation we are discussing. The second reason is more complex. We like the terms. Not only are they simple and descriptive, but they have very positive connotations for us. Between us, we have a total of over thirty years in the fund-raising field; one of us (Tempel) is and has been a fund raiser for more than twenty years. We know a lot of fund raisers, and we know that the kind of fund raising we talk about in this book is a complex, multifaceted, multistep, honorable process with complex goals and objectives far beyond a bottom-line dollar figure. We use the term inclusively, to mean those whose work involves acquiring private financial support. All such people may or may not be engaged in direct solicitation of funds. We use the terms *fund raiser* and *fund raising* with pride, affection, and a great deal of respect. We wish more fund raisers had as much reason as we have to feel the same way about these terms.

A separate but related choice we have made is to refer throughout this book to the fund-raising field, rather than the fund-raising profession. This research was born out of the desire of the Research Committee of the NSFRE Foundation to assist the field both to be seen as and to become more professionalized. According to the scholarly connotations of the term *profession*, fund raising is not likely to become a true profession like medicine or law. Fund raisers will never have the autonomy of doctors, for instance, and fund-raising work will never derive from the base of systematic knowledge that true professions have. Furthermore, when fund raisers refer to fund raising as a profession or say they want it to become a profession, they do not mean to say fund raising is or can be, strictly speaking, like medicine. Instead, what they convey is an expectation that fund raising will be both carried out and perceived as a function characterized by the public's highest expectations and standards of ethical behavior, interpersonal relationships, and excellence in performance. We sincerely hope this book will acknowledge those who already meet those expectations and encourage those who aspire to them.

Snapshots

The research presented in this book was designed to describe fund raisers and the values and knowledge they bring to their work, the things that motivate and discourage them, and the strengths and weaknesses they see in the field. Using the data collected in this research, we hope to demonstrate that fund raisers in general are well-educated, talented, committed, competent people who have a strong mission orientation and who bring strong professional and ethical values to their work. In following chapters, we present raw data from the research and observations and interpretations of the data. The verbal snapshots that follow in this chapter—like the ones in Chapters Two through Eight—describe some of the actual people interviewed for this research, providing examples of fund raisers whose career experiences illustrate the issues under consideration.

To bring our overview of the nonprofit environment to life, here we present four interviewees who have in common the general occupational title of fund raiser. They share many of the same values and personal characteristics as well as considerable knowledge about the practice of fund raising. Nonetheless, they followed very different paths to fund raising and worked in very different environments. Taken together, their experiences suggest the diversity both of the kinds of people who work as fund raisers and the environments in which they work. They are, in our opinion, a few examples of the best the field has to offer—strong people with considerable knowledge and skills, strong values about doing good things, and equally strong needs to find personal satisfaction in their work.

Nice Girls Don't Work—They Volunteer

Marlene was a sixty-five-year-old woman who worked in the nonprofit sector for forty-five years, twenty-five years as a volunteer, and twenty as a paid staff fund raiser. Although she graduated from college, she had no career aspirations because she had been taught that "nice girls don't work." While raising her children, she volunteered for organizations such as the Junior League, Planned Parenthood, the arts council, the ballet, and the neighborhood family services agency. This was an acceptable part of the affluent, suburban lifestyle in her community, and, she said,

> Frankly, that was where the fun and the action were. Doing public relations for the charity horse show and driving Davy Crockett around when I had four little boys in coonskin hats in the back seat certainly was a lot more fun than staying home. . . . There were [also] ample opportunities—and, in the absence of a career, the only opportunities—to bring your resources to the table, to learn and grow.

In 1973, after the breakup of her twenty-five-year marriage, she decided to seek a paying job. Because of her community involvement and a reputation for getting things done, she secured the position of director of the city's community foundation, her first paid position, at the age of forty-five. She then worked in fund-raising positions in two other nonprofit organizations before moving to her present organization, a national public benefit agency, where she had been for ten years. As vice president for development, Marlene developed fund-raising strategies and contacts, helped to galvanize the board, and created proposals and program budgets.

She continued her extensive volunteer activities and had an impressive knowledge of the nonprofit sector, especially regarding the mutual relationships between nonprofit organizations and private foundations. She had no plans to retire and predicted, "I will stay here until they carry me out." She viewed her professional career with considerable satisfaction, but if she had been oriented to pursuing a career as a younger woman, she thought she would now be "a big-time financial planner making a lot more than $68,000 a year."

Giving Back

Quentin's warmth and energy filled his big, cluttered office as he roamed around the room during the interview. His voice was powerful, his accent profoundly New England, his laughter full-bodied. When he was well into a career in rehabilitation services, he started thinking about a job in public relations. He said,

> Although I liked rehab, I was too far away from clients and I didn't like that. I found myself speaking to personnel managers, to Rotary clubs and parents' groups, and I thought I should probably get into public relations because that's what I seemed to be doing and I liked that. I started looking and got a lot of rejections in that area.

Eventually, he accepted the position in public relations and development at the community hospital where he currently worked and ultimately was promoted to the position of vice president. He had been there for eleven years. His staff consisted of two support persons and a raft of volunteers. He liked it that way. He said:

> I'm the chief cook and bottle washer. I do it all. I love what I do and I do what I love. I love putting all the pieces together, especially getting people to work with me. Some board people will tell me, "This person will never serve as the chairman of the campaign," and I say, "Oh, no?" I love getting on the phone talking to people, going out visiting people, working late at night, coming in early. Sometimes I schedule myself too closely and I have to run from one thing to the other and change outfits as I go, but I do it, and I love it.

An aggressive fund raiser with a strong orientation to the bottom line, Quentin admitted that playing golf with a prospect in the hope of coming back with a $25,000 check was more important to him than turning in his administrative reports on time. Although he pushed hard and asked for a lot, he expected to give back. He described his job as requiring "sometimes twenty-four hours a day," but he also wrote a weekly sports column for the newspaper, officiated at college and high school baseball and basketball games, and was active in the Rotary and the Chamber of Commerce. Quentin recounted numerous episodes testifying to his success in getting prominent people in his region to fill important volunteer positions, but he documented his success with other kinds of volunteers as well. He explained,

> There are some little old ladies who come in here who sit and stuff and label and go like crazy. You'd think they were on piecework. Sometimes I have to call them and say "The job's all done—we don't need you today," and they get mad at me! Recently, I took them out for lunch at a nice restaurant and fixed up gift packages for each of them. When I started to thank them, I started crying. I am so grateful for these people.

Quentin was deeply touched by people's generosity to the hospital. He told the story of one woman, Hazel, who called one day to say that she wanted to give $2,500 for the new building. Hazel was a seventy-eight-year-old single woman who was a stranger to Quentin at that time. After meeting Quentin and completing a tour of the hospital, she offered to increase her gift to $10,000. Quentin, surprised and pleased, cautioned her to discuss the matter with her attorney. It was not long before he heard from her attorney, whom he also invited to tour the hospital. After the attorney visited, he called to say that Hazel now wanted to increase the gift to $25,000 and also to rewrite her will, naming the hospital as the primary beneficiary.

The story might have ended there as a success story for the hospital, but for the fact that Quentin took it personally that people gave to the hospital and he responded personally. Because of this, it was natural for him to keep in touch with Hazel. During one phone call, he noticed that she seemed depressed. He continued the story:

> I said, "I need a person like you in my office. Come in for two hours and try it. If you like it, you can stay forever. If you don't, you can leave." She was uncertain, saying she was very nervous. I said, "Look, two hours, no strings." She came in one day planning to stay two hours, but she ended up staying for four hours. That was two and a half years ago and she's been coming back ever since.

Quentin knew that Hazel seemed happier once she started to work in the development office, but he did not really know how much it meant to her until he had a conversation with a friend of Hazel's, who said to him, "You made a miracle for Hazel. Hazel doesn't take any more medication. Hazel comes to parties with me, turns on the television, and wears bright clothes again." Quentin took no credit for the role he played in Hazel's metamorphosis. Instead, he emphasized the power of giving to enhance people's lives.

Making a Difference

At fifty-two, Barbara was a tall, attractive woman who looked younger than her age. Married, with grown children, she had once been a foster mother to twelve babies. She was the director of development at a private secondary school in a small city, where she had been for three years. With an associate's degree from the community college, she had begun her career in development eight years before as a secretary in the development office at a nearby private college, where she worked for almost five years. During that time, she also began to serve on the development committee of the board at the private high school she had attended. She explained:

> They were trying to start a campaign and they didn't understand what they were getting into. They wanted to build a library for $4 million from a constituency that had never been asked for a cent. They thought they could send out letters and the money would roll in. I kept saying that they had to develop an annual fund before they started a campaign. The headmaster insisted on going ahead with the campaign and asked me to come on staff. I had to decide if I wanted to be involved. Things were so bad here that I

wasn't sure I could pull it out of the fire, but I was certain that I couldn't hurt anything, and by then, I had been seduced by this remarkable school. Helping this school survive and succeed is now my passion.

Part of Barbara's challenge at her school had been to educate all the critical constituencies about the process of fund raising, including the board and other volunteers, prospects and donors, the alumni association, and the headmaster. She said:

When I arrived, the alumni association and the development operation not only did not work together but they actually worked against each other. The alumni association had a long history and a $3-per-year dues program, which they called fund raising. They thought raising money from alumni was their territory. When I said there was a lot more potential for alumni gifts, they said it just could not be done. Well, the best thing you can tell me is that I can't do something. People have done me more favors that way than by encouraging me.

Regarding the community, Barbara said:

Rating and screening had been done so indiscreetly that many people in town were furious and had bad feelings about the school. Some volunteers had told local businesses that if they wanted to do business with the school they had to give donations. That upset a lot of people. So one of my first tasks was to mend fences with a lot of people important to the school.

Educating the headmaster was one important part of Barbara's work. She explained:

Right away I established with the headmaster that he's the star and I am the stage manager. At times he tries to put me in the spotlight. One time I drafted a letter for his signature to alumni and friends announcing a gift of $1.3 million. He inserted a paragraph saying that the gift never would have happened if it hadn't been for my work with the donor. I told him that was nice of him but it had to come out. The purpose of the letter was not to say we've got a good development director.

Being needed and making a positive difference were the most compelling motivations for Barbara. She said,

> I've been recruited for other jobs, but what keeps me here is the fact that I believe in this school so much and they really need me here. Once I was interested in an opening with an national agency. I met with the board who were all seasoned fund raisers who understood what their goals were. I knew I wouldn't have to educate them, but just coordinate for them. In an odd way, that's what made me not take the job. I didn't see the need for me there the way I am needed here. Ultimately, that's why I stay. There's so much more that needs to be done here. If I continue to feel that I'm making things better here, I have no reason to leave.

Elder Statesman

We refer to Charles as an elder statesman to emphasize his forty years in and considerable contributions to the field. He had worked in fund raising since 1952, when he was discharged from the Army. His plan was to earn a Ph.D. in history and teach at the college level. However, the president of his alma mater asked him to fill the position of director of development, and Charles's first response was "What's that?" The president explained and Charles was sold. He and the president "cut a great deal" for Charles's annual salary—$2,200 per year.

Although he did earn his Ph.D. in history and did teach freshman history for a while (at a time when he also washed windows on Saturdays for the college), during his career he worked as the chief development officer for three higher education institutions and one state university system. His résumé also included a senior position at one of the major professional organizations in fund raising; he was the first person hired to help create a prestigious national public benefit organization. Before starting his own fundraising consulting firm in the late 1980s, he worked during three different periods for nationally known fund-raising consulting firms. He estimated that he had trained "probably 250 people" who have worked in the fund-raising field, and cited this as one of his most satisfying accomplishments. In his present consulting work, he focused on developing the skills and competencies of staff fund raisers, preparing them to function without consultant services.

Charles's entrepreneurial energy and his ability to bring people together and harness and direct their energies were apparent in the interview and throughout his career. He had made lasting contributions to the advancement of the field and to numerous nonprofit organizations across the country. His fund-raising career had been rewarding to him in multiple ways. He said:

> I never got bored. I didn't have time to get bored. I'll continue
> to do this until I retire and I don't know when that will be. I've en-
> joyed my career thoroughly. I have gotten paid to meet some of the
> most interesting people in the world. What am I going to do when I
> retire? Probably read, travel, and do more pro bono work.

Critical Issues

The pervasive question about fund raisers is: Are they more like highly skilled salespeople or more like highly impassioned missionaries? This question arises from the fact that fund raising has always been and will always be characterized by "tension between fund raising as business and fund raising as mission" (Harrah-Conforth and Borsos, 1991, p. 27). Fund raisers create the bridge between the mission and the marketplace; to be successful, they must be credible in both worlds and able to balance the conflicting values of both worlds. Throughout the book, and especially in Chapter Eight, we will return to the ways in which the pervasive question about fund raisers emerges in what we believe are the crucial issues challenging and concerning fund raisers today. These issues are:

- The turbulence of the nonprofit sector, an environment characterized by increasingly restrictive economic conditions and severe public criticism
- The means of entry into the field of fund raising, certification and licensing, the education and professional development of fund raisers, and their career paths
- The role and status of women and minorities in the field
- The scope, impact, and reasons for turnover in fund raising
- The levels of compensation in fund raising and overall compensation practices

- The lack of understanding about the professional practice of fund raising
- How fund raisers are perceived, both inside and outside the field
- Accountability and ethical practice in fund raising and the regulation of fund raising.

The Nonprofit Environment

The issues and challenges facing fund raisers cannot be understood without some understanding of the environment in which they work. The rest of this chapter provides a brief general overview of this environment.

Nonprofits Under Attack

In 1990, the nonprofit sector included an estimated 983,000 organizations employing 8.6 million paid staff (6.3 percent of the total U.S. workforce) and spent $389 billion, of which $156 billion was for compensation (Greene, 1992a, p. 24). One of the sector's esteemed scholars, Dennis Young (1983), wrote that in times of economic prosperity, the most scrutinized aspect of nonprofit organizations is how well they respond to public need. In more difficult economic times, Young noted, concern shifts to how much money nonprofits spend. Therefore, because of worsening economic conditions, the 1990s were destined to be a time of greater public scrutiny of nonprofit spending, but two other events ensured not only increased scrutiny but harsh criticism as well.

In February 1992, the United Way of America forced William Aramony to resign in response to public outrage regarding his $463,000 annual salary and revelations about his management practices and lifestyle (Millar, 1992). Some observers believed this event, often called "the United Way scandal," did more to diminish public regard for nonprofits than any other in recent history.

Another event, though not as well-known to the general public, precipitated vigorous scrutiny of fund raisers and nonprofit organizations by legislators and regulators. In the late 1980s, Watson and Hughey, a for-profit fund-raising firm now doing business as Direct Response Consulting Services, conducted numerous fund-raising solicitations for eight charities. These solicitations informed recipients that they were winners in a sweepstakes and asked them for a charitable donation. The cash winnings were actually quite small, as little as ten cents in some cases. Outraged callers flooded the telephone lines of consumer protection offices. The two congressional hearings and multiple investigations that followed revealed, among other things, that the company retained partial ownership of donor lists developed by the mailings. The company, which profits from renting and exchanging mailing lists to other charities, was sued by twenty-two states and came under scrutiny by both the Internal Revenue Service and the U.S. Postal Service (Williams, 1993). As a result, state legislators all over the country introduced new fund-raising legislation. If the United Way scandal captured public attention, the Watson and Hughey case became "a seminal moment in fund-raising regulation because the scale of the sweepstakes was so enormous" (Bush, 1994, p. 30).

There was widespread concern about how these events would affect philanthropic giving, and concerns were justified initially—in 1992, gifts to United Way campaigns dropped by 4.1 percent. Giving to United Way campaigns began a slow recovery, with a 0.23 percent increase in 1993 and an additional 1 percent increase in 1994 (Dundjerski, 1995, p. 27). Therefore, it appears that the long-term effect on giving of the United Way scandal may not turn out to be as negative as some had originally feared, although the continuing effects of increased public and official attention are more lasting. For many in the general public and in legislative and regulatory agencies, these events have led to concerns about the accountability and trustworthiness of fund raisers, fund-raising efforts, and the nonprofit sector overall. Many knowledgeable observers have noted that these events raise serious questions about the accountability of the boards charged with the governance of nonprofit organizations.

There were other well-known cases (such as those involving Covenant House, Jim Bakker, Stanford University's use of questionable expenses to construct its indirect cost rate for federal research funds, and more recently, the misuse of funds at the NAACP and the bankruptcy of the Foundation for New Era Philanthropy) that diminished the nonprofit sector in the public eye. There were also less notorious but numerous other cases of false reporting and diversion and waste of contributions, as well as misleading and increasingly prolific fund-raising appeals. Officials in several states have investigated and reported on the activities of for-profit solicitation firms. (These are firms that conduct direct solicitations on behalf of nonprofits and are to be distinguished from for-profit consulting firms that do not handle gifts and from nonprofit organizations soliciting on their own behalf. Distressing to many in the field is the fact that newspapers usually refer to these paid solicitors as "professional fund raisers.") Daily newspapers frequently report that many for-profit solicitation firms pass along to charities far less than half of the total raised. Reports of this kind rarely distinguish among types of fund-raising organizations. Additionally, these reports rarely make any attempt to explain the dynamics of fund-raising costs. The result is that the public receives an overall negative and very confusing picture of groups conducting fund-raising efforts throughout the nonprofit sector.

One observer (Nielsen, 1993) noted that the increase of incidents which besmirch the entire nonprofit sector are signs that "the sleaze and greediness so evident in other sectors of American life have penetrated the fields of charity, religion, education, and philanthropy" (p. 57). These events involve, at best, the misuse of funds and, at worst, actual theft—all leading to the diversion of funds away from the amelioration of public need, the erosion of public trust, and the presentation of an increasingly troubling series of images of the nonprofit sector to the public. As a result, the actions of nonprofits have become a topic of public conversation, sustained by negative coverage in the public media, which is variably accurate and well-documented but usually dramatic in its presentation. Unfortunately, the nonprofit sector has not been particularly effective in response.

One vivid example of the failure of the nonprofit sector to respond effectively occurred on the *Phil Donahue Show* on December 6, 1993, in an episode titled "Charities Don't Really Help." Panelists on that broadcast included Theresa Funiciello, author of *Tyranny of Kindness* (a 1993 book about welfare reform), Thomas Garth, president of the Boys and Girls Clubs of America, and Christine Vladimiroff, president and CEO of Second Harvest. Funiciello stated that "giving money to charities is like handing out snowballs in a blizzard. . . . A whole lot of charities are pretending to repre-

sent the interests of poor people but they're really only representing themselves. They make a ton of money. They live pretty well.
Meantime, poor people get poorer every year" ("Charities Don't
Really Help," 1993, p. 1). Funiciello said that charities should give
cash directly to the needy. Donahue responded by saying that officials are afraid that recipients would spend the cash "on Bud-
weiser." Funiciello countered with the charge that charity officials
want the cash to use it to pay for "champagne fund raisers." She
also noted that taxpayers subsidize charitable donations at great
cost to government coffers, and charities are not regulated and not
accountable in any effective way to taxpayers or to the government.

Garth, apparently in an effort to defend the quality of service
delivered by nonprofits (which was not where criticism was directed), stated that the Boys and Girls Clubs conducted a survey
to determine that alumni of the clubs were satisfied with the service they received. His point about the satisfaction of his clients
looked like an attempt to deflect attention away from criticism of
spending by nonprofits and was lost when he was prompted to acknowledge that he earned $185,000 in annual salary and the sur-
vey cost $175,000 to conduct. Funiciello stated that Second
Harvest receives large quantities of nonfood items, such as meat
tenderizer, meat marinade, mint jelly, and shoe polish, for which
corporations take large charitable deductions, and which Second
Harvest "trashes" at its own expense, a point Vladimiroff did not
address. These nonprofit executives appeared pained that their
motives and the good works of the nonprofit sector were under
attack. They did not present an articulate or compelling defense
of the nonprofit sector nor did they acknowledge the truth in any
of the criticisms leveled against the nonprofit sector, making their
embarrassed objections to inaccurate interpretations seem self-
serving and shallow.

In the past, the press may have been uncritical of the nonprofit
sector and too quick to praise, as several observers have noted. Perhaps as a sign that it is a new time for nonprofits, the *Philadelphia
Inquirer* published an investigation of nonprofit organizations in a
series of seven articles (April 18, 1993, through April 24, 1993).
This newspaper series was probably the most extensive, detailed,
and comprehensively negative coverage of the nonprofit sector to
appear in recent times in a daily newspaper. The series outlined

facets of the nonprofit sector not often discussed within the sector. For example, the series cited that:

- Nonprofit organizations control property, cash, and investments worth more than $850 billion.
- Nonprofits receive tax exemptions that result in more than $36.5 billion a year in lost tax revenue.
- The amount of charity (defined as programs and services for the poor) provided by many large nonprofits is small—in 1990, free medical care amounted to 6 percent of health care expenditures; higher education institutions spent 7 percent of their own money on student aid; and large foundations spent about 5 percent of their wealth on charitable activities.

Unaccustomed to such negative press, many in the nonprofit sector reacted defensively, while others insisted that the problem was that the nonprofit sector was misunderstood and the solution was a more effective public relations campaign. One observer (Eisenberg, 1993), concluding that the need was for significant internal change in the sector itself, wrote that the current problems in the nonprofit sector grow out of complex and multiple factors—"the cumulative result of deep federal cutbacks, tough economic conditions, benign neglect of the press, the absence of serious federal regulation, corporatization of the nonprofit sector with high salaries and perquisites, questionable ethics, a value system giving weight to growth and bigness, and finally, the unwillingness of charities to police their own activities" (p. 42).

Independent Sector (1993), in a thoughtful response to the *Philadelphia Inquirer* series, indicated that while there were "some notable problems" in the series (for example, that charities are defined as only those services provided free of charge to the poor, and the implication that charitable organizations should be run on a shoestring by volunteers or poorly paid staff), the series raised valid questions that the sector needed to consider. These questions included:

- Has the enormous growth of the sector benefitted the pubic?
- Is there a need for limitations on the ability of nonprofits to accumulate assets for future use as opposed to use for immediate public benefit?

- Should there be limits on executive compensation or closer scrutiny of expenses?
- To what extent should nonprofits use resources to benefit the poor?
- Should nonprofits support regulatory reform?

A Gallup poll revealed that the vast majority of Americans thought that greater regulation of charities was needed. Of those expressing concern about the trustworthiness of American charities, 61 percent were fifty-five years of age or older, which means that the persons who were the most concerned were those who traditionally have the most to give and also give the most. Those respondents who were most trusting of charities gave the least. Cited as the "most damaging" finding of the poll was that 52 percent of respondents believed that charities had become less trustworthy in the past ten years ("Gallup Poll," 1993, p. 6). Some fund-raising practices have caused public concern. Another survey, reported by Bailey (1993), indicated that many people are furious about the number of charity appeals they receive and that fund-raising appeals sometimes violate their basic sense of trust and fair play. Donors reported that they particularly resented appeals designed to look like invoices, appeals by telephone, and expensive-looking printed appeals. A relatively recent development in the professional literature (Goss, 1994) is a "flurry of studies" promising to shed light on donors' motivations for giving. Goss indicated that although donors said they liked knowing that fund raisers wanted to understand them better, they worried that this kind of market research could "cheapen philanthropy's lofty traditions" and that the time and money spent studying donors could be better spent elsewhere (p. 15).

As Young (1983) noted, in tough economic times, experts worry about the financing of nonprofits and most agree that nonprofit executives cannot expect private philanthropy to fill the budget gaps created by cutbacks in government financing and increasing costs (Blumenstyk, 1993). According to *Giving USA*, charitable giving in 1994 amounted to $129.9 billion, a 3.6 percent increase over 1993 (Kaplan, 1995). Under the best of circumstances, however, fund raisers do not expect to see a return to the philanthropic boom of the late 1980s, when double-digit increases in giving were common every year ("Fund Raising's Recovery,"

1994). However, a phenomenon causing optimism is that a "staggering $10 trillion" in private wealth is expected to pass from one generation to the next (Greene, Greene, and Moore, 1993, p. 1). Many fund raisers hope that a substantial portion of this amount will go to charity, either through bequests by people over fifty years of age who control the wealth now, or through later donations from "baby boomers" who will inherit the rest of the money. The speculation is that charities probably still have time to influence this transfer of wealth, even though the actual transfer of wealth to charities may not take place for another thirty to forty years.

Implications for Fund Raisers

In the 1990s, critical factors in the nonprofit environment have profound implications for fund raisers. These factors include:

- Increased scrutiny and critical judgments of nonprofit management and spending
- More donor solicitation with a corresponding increase in donor sophistication and awareness
- Greater dependence on private support for many nonprofit organizations and more competition for philanthropic dollars
- The anticipated transfer of trillions of dollars in private wealth as baby boomers approach retirement age
- The growth in numbers, size, and resources of many nonprofits, and the increased complexity of managing them— resulting in, among other things, higher salaries for some nonprofit executives.

Because of these factors, the work of fund raising has never been more demanding, more challenging, or more important. Fund raisers, who create the bridge between mission and marketplace, are among those who must mediate these issues and concerns with the donative public, while experiencing increased pressure to reach higher goals with fewer resources to apply to fund raising. To strengthen the nonprofit sector, nonprofit leaders must lose their discomfort at responding to criticism and become more credible in their defense of what is good and right about the nonprofit sector, more honest about acknowledging what needs improving in the nonprofit sector, and more courageous about promoting these improvements. Fund raisers themselves must continue to expand their knowledge of the nonprofit sector and its environment; they must critically examine how their work influences their organizations, especially becoming more purposeful in examining any unintended consequences of fundraising practices.

The research reported in this book will support and inform these processes by providing information about the people who work in fund raising and what they bring in skill and professional values to their organizations.

Chapter Two

Who Are America's Fund Raisers?

After the snapshots, this chapter offers a brief review of other research on fund raisers. We then begin the presentation of our research results by describing what might be called typical fund raisers and discussing several demographic characteristics of our survey respondents. We also provide an overview of those interviewed for the study.

Snapshots

The snapshots in this chapter describe a successful fund raiser who had no college degree but taught fund-raising courses at the college level and a high-paid fund raiser who was also a philanthropist.

Top of the Field, No Formal Education

Miriam, an elegant woman in her fifties, was the vice president for development at a prestigious health research institution. She currently earned over $100,000 per year. Miriam had no formal education beyond high school and secretarial training. Unlike many others who entered fund raising "by accident," Miriam was systematic and purposeful in seeking a career in the field. When she was thirty years old and her children were in school, she returned to secretarial work in a position she described as "a job, not a career." She sought career counseling from her former pastor, who happened to work at that time as a vice president for development for a nearby college. After Miriam described what she saw as her chief strengths—organizational skills and working with and influencing people—her former pastor suggested she consider fund raising, about which she knew nothing. Soon after, she secured a position as assistant in the development office of a private college, where she worked for fifteen years, progressing to assistant director of development, to director, and, finally, to vice president of development and public affairs.

As "one of less than a handful of women" in fund raising in the early 1970s, she learned fund raising at CASE conferences and from mentors. Eventually, she was recruited by the chief executive officer of her present organization, where she had been for more than seven years. Strongly committed to "giving something back," to the field, she played a key leadership role in a professional organization in her region and taught courses in fund raising at a nearby university. Interestingly, Miriam believed that education is the most important vehicle for strengthening the fund-raising field. Deeply concerned about the future of the field, she advocated stronger professional development programs and especially a stronger role for professional organizations in accrediting both fund-raising courses and fund-raising practitioners. Although it seems unlikely that her success could easily be duplicated today with the increasingly greater emphasis on formal credentials for advancement in fund raising, Miriam's career history indicates that factors related to success in fund raising have little to do with formal education.

Fund Raiser as Philanthropist

At the time of our interview, Mitchell, who had worked in fund raising for twenty-five years, was the vice president of development at a public research university; he earned more than $150,000 per year. A deeply religious as well as practical man, he was committed to a career in fund raising because he believed in giving but also because he wanted a career with opportunities for advancement. He believed that the best people in the field are committed not only to the advancement of worthwhile causes but to the "philosophical embrace of philanthropy as a way of life"—and that it is this personal commitment that helps fund raisers to convince others to give generously. He said, "I established my life on the principle that I had to give more when I made more. Right now, I give 20 percent of my income. Each year, as my salary increased, I would ratchet it up a percent or two." He was troubled by the fact that giving as a percentage of the gross national product has not increased, in spite of the much higher number of people working in the field. He said:

> I don't think fund raising as a field has been effective in getting more people to see that giving is a way of life, that it is more blessed to give than to receive, and that to whom much is given, much is required. We have not accomplished this as a profession. Maybe it's because too many of us in the field don't believe it ourselves.

Nevertheless, indicating that he understood the realities fund raisers face, he added:

> The inherent problem is that my immediate responsibility is to bring money into this university. It's hard for me to try to educate an alumnus to give a certain percent of his income to philanthropy when what I need from him is $1,000 for our library, so the church and hospital and symphony and boys' club be damned, so to speak. It is hard for me to challenge a person to take philanthropy more seriously although I still think we have a responsibility to do that. I try to do it with some donors I meet and with staff, maybe by example, but that's hard, too, because I risk sounding arrogant or boastful.

Although he had made a comfortable living as a fund raiser, Mitchell thought too many in the field today judge their success by salary and titles, rather than by whether they are successful in increasing philanthropic giving. He said that the leadership of the field, including the professional organizations, must become stronger advocates for giving and for supporting fund raisers in maintaining philanthropic values in their own work.

Previous Research on Fund Raisers

Earlier surveys completed by professional organizations serving fund raisers influenced the design and content of our research. For summaries of this work, see Association for Healthcare Philanthropy

(1992, 1993); Turk (1986a, 1986b) and McNamee (1990a, 1990b, and 1990c) describing CASE studies; and Bohlen (1981) and Mongon (1985, 1988, 1992) for NSFRE. In addition, both CASE and NSFRE conducted new membership surveys in 1995, reported in Williams (1996) and Mongon (1995). In general, the early surveys describing basic demographic characteristics of members are invaluable contributions to the historical record of growth and other changes in the fund-raising field since the 1980s. For instance, the survey reports reflect the overall growth in the field: the 1981 report listed NSFRE membership at 2,913, and by 1992, NSFRE membership totaled 12,644. One primary way in which our research differed from these membership surveys is that we included fund raisers from all major professional organizations in one study.

Other than the demographic data compiled by professional organizations about their memberships, the only other research addressing the same topics as the present study was that published in two monographs, *Fund Raisers of Academe* (Carbone, 1987) and *Fund Raising as a Profession* (Carbone, 1989). For the first study, which focused on backgrounds and careers of fund raisers in higher education and their attitudes about their work, Carbone surveyed five hundred fund raisers who worked in member organizations belonging to CASE. Of those responding, 60 percent were male, 97 percent were white, and more than 50 percent were age forty or under. Most respondents had bachelor's degrees; 61 percent also had master's degrees and 23 percent had doctorates. Carbone found that undergraduate fields of study for these fund raisers represented traditional academic disciplines, but there was "a preponderance of education degrees at the graduate level" (p. 5).

Carbone found that 84 percent of respondents were in their present positions from one to five years and seven out of ten respondents were in their positions for three or fewer years (p. 6). Twenty percent reported they were actively seeking employment elsewhere at the time of the survey, citing as reasons desires for increased salary, more responsibility, and greater challenge. A "surprising number" (p. 9) of fund raisers in this survey indicated that they entered the field by happenstance; others identified volunteer experiences, exposure to fund raising as the result of working at other college or university jobs, or having been influenced by those already working in the field. Respondents indicated that the most important source of training for working in the field came as the result of working in a development office. Before entering fund raising, 30 percent had worked previously as faculty members or in administrative positions in higher education; 2 percent had worked in public school systems; another 11 percent came from other areas, such as the military, nursing, or government.

In his second study, Carbone noted that a review of the programs for conferences for fund raisers indicated that almost all sessions were concerned with how fund raisers can better do their jobs. This "somewhat single-minded attention to expertise on the job," he wrote, "suggests that many fund raisers have only a rudimentary understanding of what is involved in professionalism and in the attainment of stature as a true profession" (p. 8). He indicated that competence is important, but strongly emphasized that competence is not enough if "an occupational group aspires to be recognized as a 'true profession'" (p. 7).

Carbone's 1989 survey, sent to 1,750 members of three national fund-raising professional organizations, was designed to assess fund raisers' views of themselves, their colleagues, and their occupation. The focus of the survey was on the six identifying characteristics of professions. To summarize Carbone's conclusions, these six characteristics—and fund raisers' views of them—include:

- *Autonomy.* Fund raisers realize the importance of autonomy and seek it, but only those in senior positions have it.
- *Systematic knowledge.* Fund raisers do acknowledge the importance of theoretical principles in fund-raising practice, but most are convinced that these principles are best learned on the job rather than through formal educational programs.
- *Self-regulation.* Fund raisers appear to place little value on professional self-regulation.
- *Commitment and identification.* Fund raisers do not generally seem committed to fund raising as a career or to identify with it as a unique subculture.
- *Altruism and dedication to service.* Fund raisers value giving service but also identify salary and material rewards as major incentives.

- *Ethics and sanctions.* Fund raisers generally understand the importance of ethical standards and the need for sanctions but most also indicated that they do not know how standards could be monitored, what sanctions would be appropriate, or how sanctions could be administered.

Carbone concluded that at best fund raising was an emerging profession. He wrote that increasing the professional maturity of the field is the "greatest professional challenge" fund raisers face (p. 46). Regarding fund raising's status as a profession, Bloland and Bornstein (1991) noted that an important consideration is the degree to which fund raisers share skills with volunteers. They noted that "sharing expertise with amateurs considerably weakens the occupation's power to define its work and establish jurisdictional control and legitimacy" (p. 105). Similar to the professional organizations' membership surveys, Carbone's work provides invaluable historical information and also represents seminal study on crucial issues regarding the nature of the work of fund raising. We designed our study to build on these earlier works, to provide an expanded and more detailed description of fund raisers, and to explore how best to study fund raisers.

Researchers at the Oral History Research Center at Indiana University produced two important contributions to the study of fund raising. The first, completed by Harrah-Conforth and Borsos (1991), was a project that began as an effort to create an oral history of fund raising and emerged as a key work in the study of fund raisers themselves. This project involved the study of three distinct groups of fund-raising consultants: the pioneers (such as Charles Sumner Ward, Lyman Pierce, Frederick Courtney Barber, John Price Jones, George Lundy, and Arnaud Marts); the over-sixty generation (such as George A. Brakeley Jr., John J. Schwartz, Maurice Gurin, and David Ketchum); and the under-sixty generation (such as Patrick Ryan, Toni Goodale, Jane Geever, and Franklyn Cook).

The second project from the Oral History Research Center was a three-year study of the culture of American foundations as described by foundation leaders (such as Emmett D. Carson, Charles A. Johnson, Brian O'Connell, Robert L. Payton, and Homer Wadsworth) in fifty-nine taped personal interviews (Lichtenberg, 1993).

These interviews focused "on the ideas and values of the people who make philanthropy happen" (p. 2). Interviewees were "active partners in the telling, defining, and interpreting of their own culture," and the oral history transcripts "result in a body of primary sources which contribute a lively dialogue about the important issues" (p. 2) confronting the field of philanthropy today.

Typical Fund Raisers

Respondents to our survey included 955 women (54.6 percent) and 793 men (45.3 percent). Of total respondents, 1,651 (94.4 percent) identified themselves as staff of nonprofit organizations. Of the remaining 97 respondents, 78 (4.5 percent) identified themselves as consultants, and 19 (1.1 percent) as "other."

The history of organized fund raising dates back to the Community Chest campaigns shortly after the turn of the century (Bremner, 1988). From that time and for several decades thereafter, paid fund raisers were predominantly men who worked with predominantly male community and alumni leaders and male boards of directors. Women have always played important roles in American philanthropy—but not always in paid positions. Conry (1991), for instance, described women as "the backbone of American philanthropy, organizing committees, staffing campaigns, soliciting gifts, and, in most cases, offering their expertise and skills for little or no compensation" (p. 146).

Membership surveys indicate that the male-female ratio among the ranks of paid fund raisers shifted dramatically in the past decade, with the number of women increasing by more than 50 percent by 1992. For instance, female respondents to NSFRE surveys were 38 percent of the total in 1981, 43 percent in 1985, 50.6 percent in 1988, 57.6 percent in 1992, and 57.1 percent in 1995. Similarly, female respondents to CASE surveys were 38.7 percent of the total in 1982, 48.5 percent in 1986, 54.7 percent in 1990, and 53.6 percent in 1995. Although the most recent CASE and NSFRE surveys indicate that the increase of women in the field may have leveled off, to the extent that organizational membership reflects the entire population, the data indicate that women outnumber men in the field. We speculate that women outnumber men even more among the nonmember population of fund raisers.

Some of the interviewees in our study expressed opinions about the number of women in the fund-raising field. Five interviewees, all in senior positions, said the growth in the number of women in the field was good for the field. Ten other interviewees expressed concern that the field would become feminized and that overall salaries and prestige would diminish, an issue we discuss in greater detail in Chapter Five. Three interviewees, one woman and two men, expressed reservations about the increased number of women in the field because of a preference for working with men. One of them, a man, said:

> I am threatened by overachieving females. Intellectually, I believe in equal opportunities and equal pay, but I do not look forward to working for a female. In fact, I would probably choose not to accept a job where I had to report to a woman, until women in management become more like men—more direct, not prissy, able to put men at ease. It makes men nervous that women personalize everything so much.

We used the most frequent responses from our survey for women and men to present a demographic profile of what might be called typical male and female fund raisers. The typical female fund raiser was white, 42 years of age, with an undergraduate degree in education. She worked full time for an educational organization, earned less than $39,999, carried the title of director, and worked in the annual fund area of fund raising. Her average work week was about 46 hours. She entered the field at 33.5 years of age, had an average of 2.8 different positions in fund raising, and had been in her present job for 3.5 years. She worked in fund raising for 9 years and had spent an average of 3.5 years in each position. The typical male fund raiser was white, 45 years of age, with a graduate degree either in business or education. He worked full time for an educational organization, earned between $40,000 and $59,999, carried the title of director, and worked in the planned giving area of fund raising. His average work week was about 48 hours. He entered the field at just less than 33 years of age, had an average of 3 different positions in fund raising and had been in his present job for 4 years. He worked in fund raising for 12 years and had spent an average of 4.3 years in each position. Both the typical female and male fund raisers in our study intended to stay in fund raising and to stay with their present organizations. The typical female fund raiser learned fund raising primarily through on-the-job training and experiences, while the typical male fund raiser learned fund raising primarily through professional development programs. Our study and the most recent CASE and NSFRE surveys all indicate that the typical male and female fund raisers are older now than they were a decade ago and have more years' experience in the field. These findings reflect the way the field, which grew so rapidly during the 1980s, is maturing.

Demographics in Detail

The typical depictions, presented to summarize general characteristics of those we studied, should not be taken to mean that fund raisers are a homogeneous group. To the contrary, as data presented throughout the book will indicate, this study confirms that fund raisers are highly diverse in many aspects (but, unfortunately, not racial origin). We are aware that many would like to see research results that clearly define the characteristics of the most effective fund raisers to assist in hiring and promotion decisions. One reason this request is almost impossible to respond to is that what constitutes effective performance in fund raising varies across types and sizes of nonprofit organizations. Definitions and measurements of effective performance in fund-raising programs vary with varying organizational fund-raising goals, capacity and resources for generating private support, and history of formal fund-raising programs. Another critical factor can be the degree to which a fund-raising program depends on staff or volunteers. Perhaps the most critical factor is the degree to which fund-raising results reflect fund-raising potential. For Organization A, raising $100,000 for the annual fund may qualify as unprecedented success, while for Organization B, raising $1,100,000 for the annual fund means it was a bad year. No empirical data exist to document whether it takes different skills or more skills to raise the record-breaking $100,000 for Organization A or the disappointing $1.1 million for Organization B.

In addition, the culture and personality of a nonprofit organization and of its donor constituencies can help define what personal characteristics are necessary for fund raisers to be effective in a particular environment. In some organizations, the senior administrative staff might believe that a soft-spoken, low-keyed fund raiser, with the appearance and demeanor of a tweedy academic, will be more suitable than an extroverted, energetic fund raiser with the appearance of a successful corporate executive. Therefore, instead of a specific profile, what we have to present is a kaleidoscope of images, sometimes confusing exceptions to the rules, and interesting divergences from the conventional wisdom, all supporting our belief that since nonprofit organizations differ so widely, every hiring decision must be based on a careful and thorough analysis of the needs and character of the specific employing organization.

Minorities

Unlike the major changes in the growth of the field and the shift in the gender of fund raisers in the last decade, there has been no significant change in the ethnic background of fund raisers, at least among fund raisers who join professional organizations. Fund raisers in professional organizations continue to be predominantly white. In both the 1982 and 1990 CASE surveys, minority respondents represented 4.5 percent of the total but grew to 5.6 percent in 1995. In the earlier NSFRE surveys, minority respondents represented 1.8 percent, 2.7 percent, and 9.9 percent, respectively, of the total respondents. Minority respondents in the 1995 NSFRE survey represented 17 percent of the total, but this increase reflects the fact that the sample of NSFRE members surveyed was selected to include eight hundred minority members. All but seventy-one (4.1 percent) of the respondents to our survey were white. Among these, twenty-eight were African American, nine were Asian American, ten were Hispanic, seventeen were Native American, and seven were "other." The continuing dearth of minorities in fund-raising was troubling to some fund raisers participating in this research. One fund raiser said his biggest concern about the field is the scarcity of minorities. He explained that he knew of a local chapter of his professional organization with "800 members that includes no Asians, two blacks, and no Hispanics—in one of the most cosmopolitan cities in the United States, a city where Anglos are in the minority."

Education

In general, male respondents had a higher level of formal education than female respondents. Seventy-three percent of male respondents had education beyond the undergraduate degree while only 44 percent of female respondents did. Of the 154 persons with doctorates or law degrees, 112 or 72.7 percent were men. Only 112 respondents (6.4 percent) did not have college degrees. Most of those without degrees (93 or 83 percent) were women. The five most frequently reported fields of study for women were education, business, English, management, and communication, in that order. For men, the five most frequently reported fields of study were business, education, management, law, and the ministry. When we sorted all reported fields of study into academic areas of the humanities, the natural sciences, the social sciences, and occupational or professional studies, 64 percent of all respondents (57 percent of women and 71 percent of men) had concentrated on occupational or professional studies, 21 percent of respondents concentrated on the humanities, 14 percent on the social sciences, and only 1 percent on the natural sciences. These results will be disheartening to those who believe that a broad liberal arts education is the ideal academic preparation for fund raisers.

Where Fund Raisers Work

America's nonprofit sector is an amalgam of over one million highly diverse organizations (Kaplan, 1995) including schools; hospitals; social service organizations; advocacy organizations; civic, social, and fraternal organizations; arts and cultural organizations; foundations; and religious institutions. In 1990, there were 8.7 million paid employees in the nonprofit sector (Hodgkinson and Weitzman, 1992), including a significantly higher percentage of women and African Americans than there were among all American employees combined. Women, who make up about 46 percent of all employees in the United States, constitute more than two-thirds (69 percent) of employees in the nonprofit sector. While African Americans make up 11 percent of all U.S. employees, 14 percent of all employees in the nonprofit sector are African American (p. 8). As indicated earlier, although women are now estimated to account for more than 50 percent of all fund raisers, there are proportionately fewer women in fund raising than the number of women in the nonprofit sector overall. There are proportionately far fewer African Americans in fund raising than in the nonprofit sector overall.

There is no certain way to determine how many people work as fund raisers, but we estimate that about 25,000 individuals are members of the major professional organizations for fund raisers and that there could be as many as 25,000 others working in fund raising. Fund raisers working in religious organizations are particularly underrepresented in professional fund-raising organizations.

Our study surveyed a stratified random sample of 2,501 members of professional organizations. This sample was designed to represent the estimated proportions of fund raisers working in the various subsectors of nonprofit organizations. Table 2.1 shows the areas of the nonprofit sector in which survey respondents reported working. A total of 73.6 percent of all respondents worked in education (49.7 percent) and health (23.9 percent) organizations. Those working in education and health included 68.7 percent of all female respondents and 79.5 percent of all male respondents, indicating that fund raisers working in human services, the arts, religion, public benefit, and environment are more likely to be female than male. Of the total 462 respondents not in education and health, 299, or 64.7 percent, were female. The Female-Male ratio column indicates the ratio of females to males that takes into account the overall higher number of female respondents. If the proportions of men and women in each subsector were equal, the ratio would be 1.20, which is the overall ratio of female to male respondents for this item, meaning there were 1.20 female respondents for every one male respondent. Any ratio larger than 1.20 indicates women are overrepresented, while any ratio smaller than 1.20 indicates women are underrepresented. As the table indicates, men and women were almost equally represented in health and slightly underrepresented in education and religion. The largest difference in representation of women and men was in arts and culture, where women outnumbered men by more than three to one. We think the differences are a result of the fact that women are more likely to work in organizations paying lower salaries, rather than indicating actual gender preferences for certain kinds

Table 2.1. Respondents by Nonprofit Subsector.

Subsector	Total Number	Total Percent	Female Number	Female Percent	Male Number	Male Percent	F-M Ratio
Arts and culture	93	5.4	71	7.4	22	2.8	3.23
Public benefit	32	1.8	23	2.4	22	2.8	2.55
Environment	16	0.9	11	1.2	5	0.6	2.20
Human services	204	11.7	130	13.6	74	9.3	1.76
Other	73	4.2	43	4.5	30	3.8	1.43
Health	418	23.9	225	23.6	193	24.3	1.17
Education	869	49.7	431	45.1	438	55.2	0.98
Religion	43	2.5	21	2.2	22	2.8	0.95
Total	1,748	100.0	955	54.6	793	45.4	1.20

of nonprofit organizations. As indicated earlier, only seventy-one or 4.1 percent of survey respondents reported ethnicity as other than white. Of these, forty-eight (68 percent) worked in education and health.

Although the nonprofit sector is often spoken of as a single entity, there is enormous variation among kinds, sizes, and purposes of individual organizations in the sector. This research indicates that fund raisers who work in different subsectors of nonprofit organizations are not very different from fund raisers in other subsectors in basic demographic characteristics.

Education by Nonprofit Organization

Table 2.2 displays respondents' educational levels by nonprofit subsector. The most frequent level of education is the college degree for those working in all subsectors. Of the 112 fund raisers without college degrees, 49 (44 percent) work in health. Of these, 38, or 76 percent, are women. Of the 153 respondents with doctoral or law degrees, 106 (69.3 percent) work in education. Of these, 77, or 73 percent, are men.

To determine if educational preparation differed among fund raisers from different subsectors, we looked at respondents' educational fields, which are reported in Table 2.3. Fund raisers who studied in occupational or professional fields (such as business, nursing, or teaching) were in the majority in each type of organization. Fund raisers in arts organizations included roughly equal proportions of those studying for occupational or professional fields and the humanities (such as art history, theater, or languages). The highest concentration of fund raisers who studied the social sciences (such as political science, psychology, or sociology) were in human services and public benefit organizations.

Of those who studied the humanities, the highest percentage of fund raisers worked in the arts and the lowest percentage worked in human services. Of those who studied the social sciences, the highest percentage of fund raisers worked in human services and the lowest percentage worked in the arts. These findings indicate continuity for some fund raisers between college studies and areas of occupational interest.

Table 2.2. Level of Education by Nonprofit Subsector.

	Total	High School/ Some College		College Degree/ Some Graduate		Graduate Degree		Doctoral Degree	
		Number	Percent	Number	Percent	Number	Percent	Number	Percent
Arts and culture	91	7	7.6	47	51.6	34	37.4	3	3.3
Education	862	24	2.8	386	44.8	346	40.1	106	12.3
Environment, public benefit, and religion	89	8	9.0	39	43.8	36	40.4	6	6.7
Health	406	49	12.1	207	51.0	126	31.0	24	5.9
Human services	202	20	9.9	111	55.0	65	32.2	6	3.0
Other	68	4	5.9	35	51.5	21	30.9	8	11.8
Total	1,718	112	6.5	825	48.0	628	36.6	153	8.9

Table 2.3. Educational Specialization by Nonprofit Subsector.

	Total	Humanities		Natural Sciences		Occupational or Professional		Social Sciences	
		Number	Percent	Number	Percent	Number	Percent	Number	Percent
Arts and culture	84	35	41.7	3	3.6	37	44.0	9	10.7
Education	812	196	24.1	12	1.5	470	57.9	134	16.5
Environment, public benefit, and religion	79	20	25.3	0	0.0	48	60.8	11	13.9
Health	350	78	22.3	1	0.3	221	63.1	50	14.3
Human services	176	35	19.9	3	1.7	81	46.0	57	32.4
Other	63	17	27.0	0	0.0	31	49.2	15	23.8
Total	1,564	381	24.4	19	1.2	888	56.8	276	17.6

Titles in Fund Raising

In general, job titles in fund raising usually reflect organizational position (such as director or vice president) and functional area (such as annual fund or foundation relations). Although our survey indicated that director was the most commonly reported title (for 42.5 percent of men and 51.3 percent of women), the results also indicate that there is a degree of segregation of men and women into certain organizational positions and functional areas in fund raising.

Table 2.4 shows the frequency and percentages for the most frequently reported titles reflecting organizational position for women and men, ranked by Female-Male ratio. The Female-Male ratio column indicates the ratio of females to males holding that title. (As noted in the discussion of Table 2.1, taking into account the overall higher number of female respondents, a ratio of 1.20 indicates equal representation of males and females in a given category.) As indicated in the table, some titles of higher status were predominantly held by men. Men are overrepresented in the positions of associate or assistant vice president, consultant, executive or senior vice president, president, and vice president. Women are overrepresented in the positions of associate or assistant director, coordinator, development associate, director, manager, and officer.

Table 2.5 shows the frequency and percentages for the most frequently reported functional areas for women and men, ranked by Female-Male ratio. As these results indicate, women are overrepresented in such areas as annual fund, alumni relations, community relations, foundation relations, grants, major gifts, marketing, operations and services, public relations, prospect research, special events, special programs, and stewardship. Men are overrepresented in athletics, corporate and foundation relations, endowment, external affairs, major and planned gifts, planned gifts, public affairs, and university relations.

Of the functional areas where women are overrepresented, all but the major gifts area are generally considered to be entry level or less-prestigious, lower-paying positions in comprehensive development programs. Of the functional areas where men are overrepresented, most are considered to be among the highest paying

Table 2.4. Titles Reflecting Organizational Position.

Title	Total	Female	Male	F-M Ratio
Manager	44	34	10	3.40
Coordinator	44	33	11	3.00
Officer	47	34	13	2.62
Associate or assistant director	132	88	44	2.00
Development associate	22	14	8	1.75
Director	797	473	324	1.46
Executive director	176	93	83	1.12
Assistant to . . .	16	8	8	1.00
Consultant	26	11	15	0.73
Associate or assistant vice president	43	16	27	0.59
President or CEO	59	22	37	0.59
Vice president	190	55	135	0.41
Associate or assistant dean	14	4	10	0.40
Executive or senior vice president	22	6	16	0.38
Total	1,632	891	741	1.20

and most challenging fund-raising positions in comprehensive development programs.

Although the number of women in fund raising has increased, women do not have parity with men in level of position in fund raising or, as our results will indicate, in salary, replicating the results of other recent research on the subject. Excellent discussions of the status of women in fund-raising and nonprofit organizations have been written by Odendahl and Fischer (1996) and others. In addition, other studies indicate that the issue of gender parity is complex and also help to explain how women in fund raising continue to be at a disadvantage.

Johnsrud and Heck (1994) showed that gender stratification within organizations is pervasive, persistent, and cumulative. They

Table 2.5. Titles Reflecting Fund-Raising Functional Areas.

Functional Area in Title	Total	Female	Male	F-M Ratio
Stewardship or donor relations	7	6	1	6.00
Special events	7	6	1	6.00
Special programs	14	11	3	3.67
Foundation relations	9	7	2	3.50
Grants	16	12	4	3.00
Prospect research	8	6	2	3.00
Community relations	32	22	10	2.20
Annual fund	86	59	27	2.19
Major gifts	40	27	13	2.08
Operations and services	24	16	8	2.00
Public relations	33	22	11	2.00
Marketing	20	13	7	1.86
Fund development	18	11	7	1.57
Alumni relations	59	34	25	1.36
Communications	16	9	7	1.29
Financial development	1	6	5	1.20
Corporate relations	13	7	6	1.17
Capital or campaign	33	17	16	1.06
Major and planned gifts	13	6	7	0.86
External affairs	18	8	10	0.80
Corporate and foundation relations	30	13	17	0.76
Endowment	8	3	5	0.60
Public affairs	10	3	7	0.43
Athletics	7	2	5	0.40
Planned gifts	72	20	52	0.38
University relations	12	2	10	0.20
Total	346	210	146	1.44

concluded that being female affects organizational status at the time prior to promotion and even more so at the time after promotion. The authors further concluded that being female has a powerful and cumulative impact on career advancement (p. 40) and that it may be more and more difficult to detect and prevent discriminatory actions because awareness has made discrimination less overt (p. 41). They recommended that leaders state their commitment to parity in hiring and promotion and provide the incentives and disincentives to ensure positive action (p. 41).

Some interviewees addressed the issue of the status of women in fund raising. One woman said:

The reason that bright committed women are attracted to fund raising is because the field has status and there is a sense of power in being involved in the organization's decision making. Ten years down the road, if those of us who chose the field for these reasons find we are not going to experience those benefits, we are going to be very disappointed.

Another woman said:

In fund raising, it is still clearly a man's world, which makes it harder for women to access certain circles.

A man said:

Fund raising is the least discriminatory field I am aware of. Males are still in overwhelming proportion directors of major campaigns but that's just because it reflects corporate structure.

One woman who had received a number of promotions over a ten-year period in the same organization said:

Every time I was promoted, I was given a number of new responsibilities, but the new responsibilities were always added to the ones I already had. I was always told that I was being given the opportunity to prove myself. I have observed that when men are promoted, their old responsibilities are assigned to someone else. Men are given promotions because they have proved themselves. This is the current version of the adage that women have to be twice as good to be thought of as equal.

Work Weeks and Tasks

We asked respondents to estimate the number of hours worked in an average week and, further, to identify the percent of time spent on the following tasks: internal administrative tasks; direct gift solicitation; constituent relations; proposal preparation; events; volunteer solicitation, management, and support; out-of-town travel; and others. Overall, all respondents who worked full time worked an average of 46.6 hours per week. All women who worked full time worked an average of 48.4 hours per week, and all men who worked full time worked an average of 49.3 hours per week. Table 2.6 contains information on percent of time spent on various tasks for all respondents.

As indicated, respondents spent the most time on administrative tasks and the least time on "other" tasks and on proposal preparation. Other analyses showed that women spent slightly more time than men on administrative tasks, proposal preparation, events, and volunteers; and men spent slightly more time on solicitation, constituent relations, and travel. For both men and women, percent of time spent on administration and travel in-

Table 2.6. Percentage of Time Spent on Tasks.

Tasks	Total Percent
Administration	33.1
Constituent relations	16.0
Solicitation	12.6
Volunteers	11.3
Events	8.4
Travel	7.8
Proposal preparation	6.9
Other	3.9
Total	100.0

creased slightly as salary level increased, and time spent on proposal preparation, events, and volunteers decreased. There were no other notable differences in time on task by salary level or by type of nonprofit organization.

Philanthropic Contributions and Volunteer Activities

Among respondents to this survey, 95.7 percent made philanthropic contributions and 82.4 percent engaged in volunteer activities for some organization other than their employer. A total of 79.2 percent reported both making philanthropic contributions and engaging in volunteer activities. These numbers compare very favorably to the general population—among all Americans, members from an estimated 46 percent of households both make philanthropic contributions and engage in volunteer activities (Hodgkinson and Weitzman, 1992); 72 percent of households make philanthropic contributions and 51 percent have members engaged in volunteer activities.

Among contributors in the general population, the average philanthropic contribution was about $900 or 2.2 percent of income. In our study, female fund raisers contributed between 3 percent and 6.1 percent of income and male fund raisers between 3.8 percent and 7.2 percent of income. Men at each salary level in our study contributed, on the average, about $750 more than women at the same salary level. Among the general population, the average number of volunteer hours for those who volunteered was about 18 per month. In our study, women volunteered about 17.5 hours per month and men about 16.4 hours. Men at salary levels below $80,000 volunteered on the average more hours per month than women, while for those with salaries above $80,000, women volunteered more hours per month than men. Only 1.3 percent of our respondents reported no voluntary activities and no contributions to philanthropic organizations. Clearly, fund raisers contribute money to philanthropy at a higher level than the general public, but they are about average in the volunteer hours they contribute. Their high average work weeks might not allow them to be more generous than the average in volunteering, but it is clear that they practice philanthropy themselves while engaging others in philanthropy on behalf of their organizations.

Overview of Interviewees

As a follow-up to the survey, Duronio conducted personal interviews with eighty-two survey respondents to collect additional information about fund raisers' backgrounds and careers, their attitudes about their work, and their thoughts about the strengths and weaknesses of the field.

Interviewee Selection

We asked survey respondents to indicate if they would be willing to be interviewed for this study; 946 or 54.1 percent said yes. As described in the Preface, we selected nine areas of the country where high numbers of respondents were concentrated. From respondents willing to be interviewed in each part of the country, we selected people to assure representation in the interview sample of men and women from all types of nonprofit organizations, salary levels, and length of time in the field. We specifically tried to include respondents indicating ethnic minority.

Forty interviewees (48.4 percent) were women; 42 (51.2 percent) were men. Seventy-seven interviewees (93.9 percent) were white. Of the remaining interviewees, two were African American women, one was an African American man, and two were East Indian women. Interviewees held positions ranging from senior to entry level. Salary levels of interviewees ranged from below $40,000 to above $100,000, with 90 percent of women earning less than $80,000, while only 59.6 percent of men earned less than $80,000. However, as a group, men had almost twice the total experience in the field, with an average of 16.6 years' experience, compared to the average of 9.4 years' experience in the field for women.

The average age for all interviewees was 47.4 years. For men, the range was 29 to 72 years and the average was 48.9 years. For women, the range was 26 to 65 years and the average was 45.7 years. Fourteen (eleven men, three women) had always worked in fund raising, and all of these had had fund-raising positions in at least two different organizations. The remaining sixty-eight listed 130 former occupations (54 different occupations in all) for an average of 1.7 former occupations per interviewee. Nineteen had worked in teaching, the most common former occupation. Six interviewees each had worked in banking, nonprofit administration, and sales.

About 60 percent of interviewees planned to change jobs to seek career advancement at some point in the future; the remainder had no plans to change jobs. Seeking advancement in fund raising probably would involve moving to some other organization for twenty-four of the twenty-five who intended to change jobs. Of the interviewees in this category, a total of nine (four women, five men) said they aspired to the level of vice president in fund raising.

Those who said they planned to retire from their present organizations ranged in age from 48 to 72 years, with an average age of 59.8 years. About 30 percent of the entire group had fewer than an average of three years' stay per organization, about 40 percent had three to five years' stay, and 30 percent had more than an average of five years' stay per organization. Twenty-four interviewees (thirteen women, eleven men), or 29.3 percent of the total, had an overall average of less than three years' stay per organization. Eight (five women, three men) of these had less than five years' experience in the field, leaving sixteen persons or only 19.5 percent of the study group with career histories that might be perceived as problematical in relation to turnover. However, eight of these sixteen had been in their present positions for three years or more.

Subjective Evaluations

To provide some general observations, Duronio subjectively rated interviewees using a scale of 5 (high), 3 (medium), or 1 (low) on the following characteristics:

- *Personal ambition.* Has this person's career been characterized by a strong interest in personal advancement?
- *Knowledge of fund raising.* Did this person appear to be knowledgeable about the fund-raising field?
- *Warmth.* Was this person pleasant, friendly, comfortable to be with?
- *Authenticity.* Did this person sound credible and appear to be trustworthy?
- *Communication skills.* Was this person articulate, well-spoken, and expressive?

- *Intensity for organization.* Did this person appear to have passion for his or her organization?
- *Intensity for fund raising.* Did this person appear to have passion for fund raising?

The results of these subjective evaluations appear in Table 2.7. As the table indicates, the majority of interviewees were rated high on all factors. Ratings for high ranged from 90 percent for "intensity for fund raising" to 52 percent for "personal ambition."

Since it is reasonable to assume that most people who would volunteer to spend two hours talking about fund raising would have a strong interest in the work, it is not surprising to find a high degree of "intensity for fund raising" among the interviewees. Somewhat more surprising was the high degree of "intensity for organization" among the interviewees; most interviewees had strong feelings about the missions of their organizations and the organizations' capacity to achieve those missions. Of the eleven not given high ratings in this area, three had recently lost their jobs and four were planning career changes. It was clear that the remaining three perceived their present positions as stepping stones to other jobs.

For the 79 percent with high ratings, caring deeply about the organization was an important part of the work. Over and over again, these interviewees said, "I couldn't do this work for an organization I didn't believe in or respect," or, "I wouldn't work this hard if I didn't care about this organization." For most of these thoughtful people, a strong and personal commitment to their employer organizations was one of the most important conditions *they* required to feel comfortable and be effective in their work. Both within and outside the field, many believe strongly that fund raisers, because of the nature of the work they do, should have more organizational commitment than might be expected or required from other staff. Far less frequently discussed is the idea that fund raisers may require and expect more of their organizations than other staff. In other words, as we describe in more detail in the section on turnover in Chapter Three, fund raisers may be more discerning and demanding employees than staff in some other areas.

The items "warmth" and "communication skills" are related, both having to do generally with how much the interviewer enjoyed being with each person and how easy the interview was to

Table 2.7. Subjective Evaluations of Interviewees.

Factor	High		Medium		Low	
	Number	Percent	Number	Percent	Number	Percent
Ambition	43	52	32	39	7	8
Knowledge of field	62	76	20	24	0	0
Warmth	53	65	26	32	3	4
Authenticity	67	82	9	11	6	7
Communication skills	70	85	12	15	0	0
Intensity for organization[a]	65	79	10	12	3	4
Intensity for fund raising	74	90	7	9	1	1

[a]Four interviewees were consultants, not affiliated with a single nonprofit organization.

conduct. The majority of interviewees were rated high on both items. These were for the most part charming, articulate people who talked and laughed easily. A few people were given other than high ratings for "communication skills" because they talked too much, or they were difficult to interview because they did not listen well or otherwise did not respond to attempts to structure the interview. Only three were rated low for "warmth," people who were quite unusual in this group.

There were no low ratings for "knowledge of fund raising." Even those with troubled career histories projected confidence and expertise. Notwithstanding résumés that document frequent job changes, it was easy to see how these people would be convincing in job interviews, perhaps especially with people who themselves were not knowledgeable about the field. Regarding "authenticity," 82 percent of the interviewees were people one might trust, hire, like to work with, or work for. The interviewer was not completely certain about the credibility of the others, because of contradictory factual statements or what appeared to be exaggerated claims of their achievements.

Fewer high ratings were given for "personal ambition" than for any other characteristic, making this the characteristic on which interviewees were most diverse. As for the forty-three (or 52 percent) interviewees who were rated high on "personal ambition," these were people whose primary motivations were to be successful in their careers, to earn progressively more money, and to have progressively more responsible positions and progressively higher status. However, it is important to note that for most of these, the definition of *successful* also included a strong emphasis on making a contribution to something beyond their own personal success, something they thought was important to society. These people would not work for organizations they did not respect and value, and many of them believed that the opportunity to have a career in the nonprofit sector was a blessing, a luxury. Because they had impressive track records, they were in demand and could and did exercise considerable judgment and discretion in making job changes. Furthermore, many of them had very high standards for their own productivity and results. One interviewee said:

It is important to care about one's work, but what pushes me to do my best are my three boys and the life my wife and I are building for them. I would sell life insurance or cars to provide for my family if I had to, but it is a real luxury to be able to do something meaningful.

This fund raiser was thirty-seven years old, had had two fund-raising jobs in eight years, earned about $65,000 as a major gifts officer for a private university, and hoped someday to move into a position of vice president for development at an educational institution. He appeared to be a principled, compassionate, competent, intelligent person and he revered the university he worked for. He worked long hours at his job and also served as an active volunteer in several community organizations. His admission that the most compelling motivation for him was to provide the best for his family clearly does not detract from his worthiness as a nonprofit employee. Does the fund-raising field need to ask any more of him and the many other professionals like him?

Because the tension in fund raising between mission and business will always be part of the excitement, the burden, and the challenge of fund-raising work, those people who have strong values regarding their own success and excellence in their work, as well as a strong desire to contribute to something beyond themselves, may be the best people working in the field.

Chapter Three

Fund-Raising Career Patterns

This chapter presents data from the research on career histories. It includes discussions of turnover in fund raising and of fund raisers who move from one subsector of nonprofit organizations to another.

Snapshots

The snapshots in this chapter include some fund raisers with long careers in fund raising, some with troubled careers in fund raising, and some who have worked in more than one kind of nonprofit organization.

Long-Timers

At sixty-one years of age, Jean was the executive vice president for development and public relations at a research hospital on the West Coast, a position she had held for more than eleven years. She earned over $100,000 per year. When her children were small, she taught part time and was involved in volunteer fund-raising activities. She was fired from her first full-time teaching position for not "doing the sort of job" the principal wanted, an event she described as the "best thing that ever happened to me because it got me out of teaching." A friend told her about a fund-raising position for a child guidance clinic, where she worked for five years before moving to another fund-raising position at a small public benefit foundation, where she stayed for three years. Her next position was as director of development for capital and planned gifts at the research hospital where she was now executive vice president.

She was interested in what deters women from trying to get to the top of their fields. She noted:

> Most women don't want the top job. They don't see themselves in that position and they don't even strive for it. I continue to be amazed by the lack of women in boardrooms. There may be a glass ceiling but there are not many women trying to break through it. The cost for women to get to these positions is very high. The costs are all at home. I fought the battle at home and won. For years my husband said I was competing with him even though I always told him I was competing with myself because I always knew I could do better. He finally understood. I make more money than he does now and he doesn't mind. He attends black-tie dinners as the dutiful spouse just as I still do for him. Having children is a big issue for women with careers. I had my children first so I didn't have to deal with the problems of interrupting my career, but child care is a big problem for women. Some husbands today will help with child care but it certainly wasn't true for me or for my friends. My friends were very critical of me when I hired a sitter and went to work. The guilt sets in and never goes away.

Martin, one of the most aggressive, energetic, enthusiastic fund raisers among our interviewees, was also the oldest. He was seventy-two at the time of the interview. He had been a fund raiser for six years, serving as executive director of a community college foundation. After a forty-two-year career in public education as a teacher, principal, and superintendent, he had scheduled his retirement. On the day before his last day of work, the president of the community college called him and said he wanted Martin to come work for him. The job was to mobilize the foundation board and improve fund-raising programs. Martin accepted the job and learned that the board had the goal of raising $20,000 that year. He thought they could raise $2 million, and they did. His goal for the current year was $11 million. Technically, his job was part time, but he worked full time; he earned $11,000—enough to cover the taxes on his pension with a little left over. When asked about his long-term career plans, Martin laughed and said he planned to retire in a few years. Although he loved the college and his work, "it's work, hard work," he said, "and there are other things I'd like to spend more time on. You'll find out when you're seventy-two that you start thinking it may be time to relax more—but I will probably be a volunteer member of the board when I do retire."

Carver, the director of major gifts at a professional school of an Ivy League university, was sixty-five at the time of the interview. In a thirty-year fund-raising career, he had worked for three higher education institutions, with a total of twenty-five years at his present institution. He had worked for the same professional school for twenty-two years. Over the years, he had "interesting offers" to go elsewhere and he seriously considered many of them. In each case, he weighed what his present job offered compared to what the new job offered. Every time, he said, "In my personal situation, overall finances, challenge, and sense of accomplishment, this place was always better. It's only been in the last few years that I have decided that I won't leave here until I retire a few years from now. You could argue that I am just a stick-in-the-mud who didn't have enough get-up-and-go to improve myself, but I have never run into anything that I thought would be as satisfying as this job."

Carver said that it was the school's alumni that made the job so challenging and satisfying. Coming from one of the most prestigious professional schools in the world, Carver's constituency included U.S. presidents and Fortune 500 CEOs. He was concerned about the increase in competition for philanthropic dollars and the negative reactions donors have to increased solicitations. He was also concerned about a trend he has observed among people with substantial means:

> I hear a lot of wealthy alumni say, "I need to preserve my assets for my children and my grandchildren. The salaries they can expect to earn are never going to buy houses and send kids to college and graduate school." I think that attitude will affect giving.

Francine, sixty-four at the time of the interview, had recently retired after a twenty-year career as the administrator of an arts center foundation. Described once in a newspaper article as "60 years old going on 29," Francine said for most of that time she did not think she would be in that position until she retired. However, she said, "As I got older and had been there longer, instead of getting restless, I kept getting more and more intrigued by the fact that we were doing so much good and still had more potential."

She reflected on the changes she had observed in the fund-raising field:

> In the 1960s and 1970s, there was no respect for fund raisers. There was no legitimacy to a career in fund raising. Beginning in the late 1970s, the professional organizations have been the most important reason for the strides the field has made. What would make me happiest would be to see the field advance to the next stage and require people in the field to have degrees in fund raising and philanthropy. Fund raising is going to be around forever and is becoming more important to nonprofits all the time. We need more and better-trained people. People aren't going to be able to pull themselves up by the bootstraps in the field the way I did.

She believed strongly not only in formal education for fund raising, but that such degree programs should be in the humanities to emphasize that interpersonal skills and compassion were required for success.

Troubled Career Histories

Among those interviewed, there were a small number of people who had what could be called *troubled* career histories—too many jobs in too few years or too many unexplained job changes. For example, three of our interviewees averaged two years per job or less over the long term—one with five jobs in ten years and another with six, and the third with nine jobs in fifteen years. The interviewee with six fund-raising jobs in different organizations in ten years was in his last week in his current job at the time of the interview. He had been in that position just over a year. He indicated that his position had been eliminated in a reorganization of fund-raising staff as a result of budget constraints. About four weeks after the interview, he wrote to say that he was in a new position and was optimistic about his future there.

It was difficult in these cases to determine the factors resulting in job changes—interviewees were not always forthcoming with details. While some acknowledged in some cases that they had been asked to leave, no one mentioned being fired for unsatisfactory performance. Interviewees cited personality conflicts, reorganizations, new administrations, and sexual harassment as some reasons for multiple job changes. None of these interviewees thought their job histories represented a problem either to them personally or to the field of fund raising, and none of them expressed concern about turnover in the field. In general, they expressed positive feelings about the field, conveyed self-confidence about their skills and abilities, and were often insightful in their understanding of the field. Interestingly, all these people had always worked in fund raising and indicated that they intended to stay in the fund-raising field.

One interviewee who had worked in senior positions had been in three organizations in ten years and was fired from the two most recent positions. This interviewee was unemployed at the time of the interview and reported that both terminations came about because the CEO in each case "did not understand fund raising." In the first termination, the CEO's lack of understanding led to unrealistic expectations about how quickly major gifts could be secured. In the second termination, the CEO's lack of understanding led to disagreements about the cultivation and deployment of volunteers in the fund-raising effort.

In many respects, interviewees with troubled career histories were quite like the other interviewees, that is, personable, bright, and articulate about fund raising. Perhaps the most important factor to note regarding those with troubled career histories is that they continue to get jobs in fund raising.

From Education to the Arts

Collette was fifty at the time of the interview, had been a fund raiser for fifteen years, and worked as director of development for the music society at a large public university. A journalist and former teacher, she had had only two full-time staff positions as a fund raiser. She went to work at a community college to write promotional materials and later accepted the responsibility for creating a private foundation for the college: "It was my baby for awhile, starting from nothing and building a board that did great things, including creating a successful scholarship program." She was in that position for ten years. During that time, because of her love of music, she served as a member of the advisory committee at the music society where she was now employed. The director asked her to apply for the position of development director. She was not considering a job change at the time, believing she needed to stay at the foundation until it was better established, but the more she heard about the job at the music society, the more attractive it sounded. Although the community college and the foundation were very important to her, she remembered a friend's comment once that every ten years or so everyone needs to be "repotted." She took the job because it would be something fresh and new, and she knew she could "speak with passion" about the case for support for the music society. She also knew that working for the music society would take her to a different world. She said, "I felt very committed to the goals of the foundation, but there was so much sorrow to deal with in that job. So many people there who needed help were in devastating situations—women who were abused and young people from seriously disadvantaged backgrounds. I was consumed by these heartrending stories, and music had always been a source of comfort and happiness." When they offered her the job more than three years ago, "it was really hard, but I was really eager to take it, and I have not been sorry," she said.

Collette found her job enormously satisfying. She explained:

The concert last Saturday was a good example. It was amazing. All 4,200 seats were filled. People stood for five encores. It was such a wonderful experience and it was really satisfying to me to know I made this happen. I felt very good about that and the best part is that it isn't sad!

Although she found exhilaration in her work, she also described the demands and pace of the job as stressful. She said:

Even though I feel tremendous pressure in this job, there are such great things that happen along the way that revive me. My days here are really, really long. This job is truly my life. I'm here early in the morning and late at night. I'm always trying to think of new ways to make things happen. This is a job that is never finished. I wake up in the night thinking about my work and I think about it driving down the street. I just don't ever forget about it. It's always in my head.

Collette definitely thought she would leave the music society one day. "Although I'm real happy here," she noted, "I think about the value of 'repotting.' I can't imagine that I'll still be here in ten years." Collette thought she might like to work for a private or corporate foundation.

From the United Way to the Arts and Back

Paula was the campaign director for the United Way in a moderate-sized city. She had been in that job for three years. It was her third job with the United Way and her fourth job in fund raising. Raising children and following her husband around the country as he pursued his career goals, she took thirteen years to finish her undergraduate degree. After graduating, she sold real estate and became a sales trainer and then worked on the staff of a candidate for Congress. After he lost the election, she went to a job placement service.

> [I told them] about my background which had this variety of places and things that didn't seem to have a lot in common. They called me later and said they had a job posting they didn't know what to do with, which they thought might be right for me, because they didn't know what to do with me, either. So they sent me to an interview at the United Way. That's when I started fund raising.

When Paula was divorced in 1985, she was earning $15,000 as a United Way campaign associate. She said:

> The director of the art museum in town had been taking me to lunch and trying to get me to go to work there for several months. I liked what I was doing at the United Way, but when she called me the week when I was first facing what I thought was terrible poverty and told me that the salary would be $25,000, I couldn't refuse. So, I went to the art museum. It was different raising money for art as opposed to the United Way. I would feel frustrated when I went to a company that would give $10,000 to the art museum that I knew had the previous year given $5,000 to the United Way, and I would think, "Art is really important but you guys have to get your priorities straight." I found myself having conflicts about what I was

doing. Also, I had little patience with the whole tea party circuit, that whole scenario of hours and hours of feeding people punch and cookies, trying to convince them to make fund-raising calls on their friends. The art museum world is more of a social world but I operated more comfortably in a more businesslike world. And, even though they hired me to improve their fund-raising programs, every time I tried to do the things they said they wanted me to do, they would say, "No, do it the way we did it last year."

She began to look for another job and left after ten months, feeling somewhat uncomfortable about "shorting the art museum by not staying a full year," to take a position with the United Way in another city. She added:

When I first came here I was given the impression that I would be heir apparent to the executive director, but now I don't think the executive director is going to leave in a few years so I think I'll go someplace else. I have enjoyed fund raising from week one and within a couple of years, I began to see that I was good at it. When I got the job offer from the art museum, I realized that I was a valuable commodity. There's a demand out there for fund raisers. I sometimes think my next move might be to a hospital. I see the income disparity between especially hospitals and social agencies for fund raisers and it would be nice to earn more money.

Renaissance Man

Tom had a twenty-three-year career in fund raising and worked in private colleges, an Ivy League university, a major public university, a renowned research institution, and one of the most prestigious art museums in the world. After earning a degree in English, Tom accepted a job working for a newly established organization that had a grant of $100,000 to create a plan for a community college system in a northern state. He was there for four years, earning $50 a week, raising money for outreach programs, until his college alma mater recruited him to raise money for them. He did that for a few years until another college recruited him for the position of director of development, where he stayed for three years. Initially, he said he had "a very good time" at the second college:

The president of the college was really a pleasure to work for. He understood that you needed to spend money to raise money. He was replaced by someone who didn't want the job, period, and who certainly was not interested in development. I was disenchanted and decided to get out of there. I applied for a job that I read about in the *Chronicle of Higher Education,* of all places.

Tom said he got this job—at a world-renowned science research institute—to his surprise and later to his dismay. He explained:

It was an interesting, wonderful institution, but it was funded by government money and research grants, which the development person had nothing to do with since the scientists wrote their own proposals. They had set a $2 million ceiling for nongovernment gifts so as not to hurt their indirect cost rate with the government. It was the kind of place that was so easy to raise money for that after about two months, even as the new guy, I had raised my $2 million and they didn't want me to do any more. I didn't have anything to do. For the next couple of months, I spent a lot of time learning about science from the best people in the field and that was very exciting, but I got very frustrated and knew I would go crazy.

He looked again in the *Chronicle of Higher Education* and learned about a job at an Ivy League university. He applied and got the job. "That was quite a move for me," he said.

Going to that university was very, very special. That's when I really knew that fund raising was my career. I enjoyed it and I raised enormous amounts of money. I still have never raised as much money as I raised there. It was just thrilling to raise a million dollars a week and I really enjoyed the people. It was fun to go to work in the morning; it was never routine. I was dealing with Nobel Laureates who treated me like a peer. I learned so much. It was so exciting to be learning from the very best people in the world who treated me as a peer.

Tom also noted that part of the satisfaction of that job was the university itself.

[It] was such an interesting place to pursue my personal interests. I got to know people in the music library who gave me wonderful things to listen to. People were the same way at the rare book library. They were really very nice to somebody like me who was sort of a dilettante, interested but not an expert, who got really excited about this stuff.

After the campaign was successfully completed, Tom got a call from the vice chancellor at a public university about a job as director of development for health sciences. Tom took the job but he said:

As it turned out, I didn't much care for my boss in development, so I just got the job done and started looking and that's how I ended up here at the museum a little more than five years ago. This is a very special place. I'm very partial to this place; I've been coming here since I was a little kid.

He noted that fund raising for the arts was more difficult than it once had been:

Donors are paying more and more attention to the homeless and AIDS. The arts used to be fun and now it's not quite politically correct or responsible for a corporation to give a million dollars to the museum when there are people living in boxes outside their corporate headquarters and they're firing employees. I don't think that's unreasonable. Interestingly, I don't think most of the people who work here think that's unreasonable. They're smarter than that and they have their priorities straight. We all think art is important but it's not the only thing. We also think that a lot of people should be able to do both and they do.

Tom said that he thought his strength in fund raising was in his communication skills. He added:

I can take something complex and make it accessible to people. It was true with science and medicine and it's true of art. I think I'm very good at explaining, at taking something that seems difficult and making it less complicated. Especially when I get excited about some things, I can make it exciting for other people. I get enthusiastic and it can be contagious. Even though I can take my skills into any nonprofit area, I couldn't work at a place where I wasn't excited about what they were doing. There are a number of things that I think are really wonderful and worthy, but I can't get very excited about them.

When asked about his future, he laughed and said:

I don't know. I just don't know. I haven't planned my career so far and I've been very lucky. Some extraordinary opportunities have come my way. I'm amazed that I got some of the jobs that I did. I sometimes think that since AIDS is killing people I know, and when I see the homeless—and you can't not see the homeless situation in New York, and there's no way that this can't affect you—it makes me wonder if maybe I shouldn't be doing more, working for causes like that. On the other hand, I have a strong passion for classical music and working in that area would be fun. I also get a steady stream of people coming to see me from all over the world, particularly Europe, who are just starting to do fund raising. I've never lived outside of this country, but it might be interesting to do fund-raising work in another country for a good organization.

Turnover

In Chapter Eight, we discuss the prevailing perceptions of fund raisers, many of them negative. One aspect of the negative perception of fund raisers concerns turnover in the field. Even though the majority of our respondents reported a high degree of commitment to stay in fund raising and to stay with their present organizations, many fund raisers who participated in this research believed that the rate of turnover among fund raisers is a problem and some respondents thought that high turnover is a reflection of fund raisers having more commitment to personal achievement than to their organizations. One interviewee said:

I get résumés from people who want to work here. Their résumés indicate that they were at the symphony for two years, at a hospital for two years, at a museum for two years, at a college for three years, and at the heart or cancer organization for two years. I don't understand how that person could have had any investment in any of those programs. I won't hire someone if I don't think that person will make an investment here, so I just toss that kind of résumé out.

Another interviewee said:

The development person should be building bridges between the
organization and its supporters. Unfortunately, we have a profession that demands one kind of behavior and professionals who
behave differently. I think the core of fund raisers today has a
me-first mentality.

Although most respondents who expressed concern about
turnover tended to hold fund raisers responsible, some interviewees saw other reasons for high turnover. One interviewee said:

A lot of fund raisers I know have moved around because they have
not felt supported by their boards and presidents. Development is
a gamble, and there are going to be bad years. There needs to be a
lot of cooperation between fund raisers and boards so that everyone buys into the fund-raising effort and, when the bad years come,
the fund raiser isn't out there alone.

Another interviewee said:

Administrators and boards are sometimes responsible for a lot
of turnover in the field. There are presidents and deans who know
that if the college raises a lot of money on their watch, it will advance their own careers. So, they look for hired guns who have
been successful at making a big hit in the short time before they
move on. It's not just fund raisers who are more interested in their
own careers than they are in the strength of the organization.

We think the scope of the turnover rate problem is overstated
and the underlying interpretation—lack of appropriate values
among fund raisers—is wrong. Our research data suggest that
turnover in fund raising is related to the rapid growth of the field,
the resulting opportunities for advancement for fund raisers, and
the strong competition for experienced fund raisers. The implication is that as growth of the field slows, the field itself will become
more stable. One measure of the growth of the field is the number
of advertisements for vacant positions. We counted the number of
ads for development positions appearing in the *Chronicle of Higher*

Education over a twenty-year period. In the month of November 1975, 18 ads for development positions appeared in the *Chronicle*. In November 1985, there were 101 ads for development positions, and in November 1995, there were 88 ads. These figures indicate the rapid growth of positions in higher education fund raising in the 1980s and also suggest that the field—and presumably, turnover in it—has become more stable.

An interesting phenomenon during the 1980s and continuing to the present is the amount of aggressive recruiting (some call it raiding) going on in the field. Many interviewees, some with long tenure in the field, said they have never been out of work, never initiated a job search, and never applied for a fund-raising position. (Unfortunately, the survey, which preceded the interviews, did not specifically collect information on this point, which is an important topic for future research.) Many interviewees reported multiple experiences of being actively recruited for particular positions and turning them down, even when to accept clearly would have been a promotion in status and salary.

Conventional wisdom maintains that long tenure and continuity of staff is a major factor in long-term fund-raising success, a corollary of the premise that long-term fund-raising success is a developmental process built on long-term relationships. Comprehensive fund-raising programs are designed to begin with annual appeals that not only bring immediate contributions but also serve to identify repeat donors. These donors can be drawn closer to the organization and may be persuaded to increase their gifts. From the ranks of repeat donors, fund raisers identify those with both the capacity and potential willingness to provide gifts of the magnitude likely to affect the organization in more enduring and more dramatic ways. These donors are singled out for the personal cultivation that oftentimes literally takes years before such donors commit to major gifts.

Fund-raising managers believe that the likelihood of major gifts is enhanced if the process is facilitated by the same development officer or other organizational representative, because the process of cultivation is often synonymous with the development of increasingly significant personal relationships between prospective donors and the organization. This holds both for individual donors and for relatively stable constituency groups (such as alumni bodies for educational institutions). Therefore, organizations value long tenure of fund raisers, not only because turnover is costly—one study indicated that turnover costs range from five to twenty-five times an employee's monthly salary (Glick, 1992)—but also because long tenure is viewed as something that increases the value of specific fund raisers to the employing organization. One interviewee related how he came to understand the value of long tenure. He said:

> When I was younger, I had some doubts about continuing in fund raising. I thought that fund raising was a very good young man's game because you get exposure to people in business and society that you don't get in many other fields; but, since the fund raiser is always somewhat subservient in the relationship, I didn't think I would want to stay in fund raising. As I imagined getting older, I didn't want to be subservient to people who were my peers in age. More recently, as I see older people in the business who have developed more comfortable relationships with people over time, I can see now that if fund raisers stay in the community over time and develop credibility they earn a level of respect that keeps them from being subservient.

This interviewee thought that nonprofit organizations had yet to learn about the value in continuity of fund-raising staff. He said:

> If our organizations started to realize the value of that continuity and adjusted compensation for that, they would get so much more value from their investment in us. Right now is a tremendous time for organizations to start investing in their futures by making sure present staff stays put.

About his own situation, he said:

> Let's say that right now I'm working with a forty-year-old physician and I have a friendly business relationship with him. I know he's paying off his house and planning on sending his kids to college. Twelve years from now, when he and I are both in our early fifties, I will say, "Arthur, the kids are through school, you're making a million dollars a year, when are you going to increase your annual gift? How about doing some estate planning and setting up a trust for the medical center?" I have tremendous potential for duplicating

that relationship with prospects I now know for the medical center all over the community. I will have a tremendous advantage over someone who hasn't worked with Arthur all those years.

There is some research indicating that turnover in advancement is higher than for some other fields. According to a study of administrative staff at CASE member institutions, the turnover rate for advancement staff was 17.3 percent, 50 percent higher than the 11.8 percent turnover found among such areas as finance and student affairs (Thomas, 1987, p. 6). Within the functional areas of advancement, turnover was higher for development (19.5 percent) than for public relations (18.2 percent) and alumni relations (13.9 percent). Fiscal affairs staff had the lowest rate of turnover (9.9 percent). About 84 percent of the turnover in advancement was voluntary and primarily related to career moves (p. 9). A more recent survey (Mooney, 1993) indicated that chief development officers and alumni relations professionals switch jobs more often than other higher education administrative staff. The study noted that 22 percent of chief development officers and alumni directors left their jobs each year and had an average tenure of 4.6 years, compared to the group with the lowest turnover, head librarians, with turnover at 11 percent and average tenure at 9 years.

Based on our findings, are fund raisers ambitious and interested in career growth? Yes. Are the majority of fund raisers transients, driven either by greed for personal advancement or failure to meet the grade? No. Do the majority of fund raisers have stable career histories? Well, not exactly, but we do not think that a lack of appropriate values is responsible for this. We think the tremendous growth of the field and the demand for experienced fund raisers are more responsible.

Fund Raisers' Career Histories

We looked at several variables related to career histories: number of jobs in fund raising, years in present job, total years in fund raising, and average years per fund-raising job. It is important to note that for survey respondents it was not always possible to tell if a job change was a promotion within the same organization or a move to another organization. In the minds of many, these are two very different kinds of changes because when fund raisers change jobs within an organization, their knowledge of and relationships with donors are retained by the organization. However, when fund raisers leave one organization to go to another, the organization may not retain those assets. To counteract this, knowledgeable fund-raising managers now try to assure continuity through keeping good records and creating many anchors for important donor relationships.

As indicated in Table 3.1, women had an average of 2.79 jobs, 8.25 total years' experience in fund raising, and 3.25 average years per job; men had an average of 3.06 jobs, 12.33 total years' experience, and 4.42 average years per job, indicating that, overall, men had slightly more job stability than women. Research indicates that persons in entry level positions change jobs more frequently (see, for example, Worth and Asp, 1994). The fact that women as a group more often work in lower-level positions in fund raising probably accounts for most of the differences in the career history data of male and female respondents.

More than half of all respondents, 55.3 percent (64 percent of women and 45 percent of men), had fewer than ten years' experience in fund raising. Job stability increased for men and women as total years in the field increased. Ten years' experience forms a significant break point. Career history patterns on each side of that line were very different from the patterns that emerged when all respondents were grouped together without regard for length of time in the field. As indicated in Table 3.1, persons with ten or more years' experience in the field had considerably more job stability than those with under ten years' experience. Given the rapid growth of the field in the past decade, the differences in career history data for various lengths of time in the field are critical to evaluating and interpreting turnover in fund raising. None of the other studies on turnover that we have seen specify length of time in the field, so there is really no way to determine if turnover for those with under ten years' experience in fund raising is excessive when compared to persons with equal tenure in other fields.

Stable, Marginal, and Transient Career Histories

After the first sort of respondents into those with ten or more years' total experience and those with under ten years, we isolated fund raisers in each group whose career histories showed evidence

Table 3.1. Career History Statistics.

Group	Number	Percent	Average Number of Fund-Raising Jobs	Average Years in Present Job	Average Years in Fund Raising	Average Years per Job
Females						
All	900	100	2.79	3.25	8.25	3.31
10 or more years' experience	324	36	3.82	4.51	14.12	4.60
Under 10 years' experience	576	64	2.21	2.55	4.98	2.60
Males						
All	764	100	3.06	4.35	12.33	4.42
10 or more years' experience	420	55	3.85	5.77	18.35	5.72
Under 10 years' experience	344	45	2.10	2.76	5.14	2.89

of job hopping. To do this, we sorted respondents with ten or more years' total experience into three groups:

- Those with an average of five or more years in each job; we called this group "+10 Stable."
- Those with an average of from 3.0 to 4.9 years in each job; we called this group "+10 Marginal."
- Those with an average of under three years in each job; we called this group "+10 Transient."

Similarly, we also sorted respondents with under ten years' total experience into the following four groups:

- Those with three to nine total years in fund raising, with an average of three or more years in each job; we called this group "−10 Stable."
- Those with three to nine total years in fund raising, with an average of under three years in each job; we called this group "−10 Transient."
- Those with under three total years in fund raising with more than one fund-raising job; we called this group "−10 Marginal.
- Those with under three total years with only one job in fund raising; we called this group "Unknown."

Table 3.2 contains a summary of this analysis. As indicated, only 540 or 32.5 percent were transients—respondents with career histories that show evidence of job hopping. Of these, 387, or 71.7 percent of the transients, had under ten years' experience. Only 153, or 28.3 percent of the transients, had ten or more years' experience in the field.

These findings indicate that most job changes were made by people with less experience in the field, and that job stability increased as people became more experienced. These findings suggest that as growth of the field levels off, and more people in the field are experienced practitioners, the rate of turnover will decrease. Furthermore, we believe that the percentage for those with stable career histories is conservative and probably too low because many job changes counted here were certain to have been promotions within the same organization, which actually indicates more stability in fund raising. In general, the findings of this study

Table 3.2. Stable, Marginal, and Transient Career Histories.

Label	Years' Experience	Years per Job	Total Number	Total Percent	Female Number	Female Percent	Male Number	Male Percent
Stable	10 or more	5 or more	281	16.9	97	10.8	184	24.1
	3 to 9	3 or more	341	20.5	199	22.1	142	18.6
	Total		622	37.4	296	32.9	326	42.7
Marginal	10 or more	3–4.9	310	18.6	130	14.4	180	23.6
	Fewer than 3	a	32	1.9	23	2.6	9	1.2
	Total		342	20.6	153	17.0	189	24.7
Transient	10 or more	under 3	153	9.2	97	10.8	56	7.3
	3 to 9	under 3	387	23.3	249	27.7	138	18.1
	Total		540	32.5	346	38.4	194	25.4
Unknown	Fewer than 3	b	160	9.6	105	11.7	55	7.2

a More than one fund-raising job.
b Only one fund-raising job.

support our position that turnover in the field is more attributable to the growth of the field and current high demand for experienced practitioners than to opportunism on the part of fund raisers.

Career Histories and Salary

Table 3.3 lists a summary of career histories for men and women at various salary levels. As indicated and as might be expected, as total years in fund raising increased, salary increased for both men and women. Job stability as indicated by average years per job also increased as salary increased (except for women in the highest salary range, whose average years per job are lower than for women in the second highest salary range).

There are some interesting differences in career histories for men and women at various salary ranges. For women earning $40,000 to $59,999, the average number of jobs in fund raising was 2.96, compared to 4.83 for men at the same salary level. This may indicate that men in this pay range changed jobs more frequently than women or that men changed jobs to get to this salary range while women were able to advance without as many job changes. For the salary range $80,000 to $99,999, women had an average of 4.12 jobs while men had an average of 3.63. Men and women earning the highest salaries had the highest average for years in present job, indicating that the highest-paid fund raisers stay put. We know from anecdotal evidence and experience that fund raisers at the top of the field are actively recruited, many receiving offers that would substantially increase their already high salaries. This suggests that the lure of the market may fail to attract after a certain point.

The NSFRE membership surveys demonstrate that there is a ceiling in salary for those who change jobs too frequently. The 1992 report (Mongon, 1992) stated that "switching employers on the average produces more pay, [but] by the time a person joins a fourth employer, however, the positive salary effects of job change diminish. With more than five employers, there is actually an inverse relationship" (p. 18). The most recent NSFRE membership study (Mongon, 1995) confirmed this finding, noting that "statistics continue to indicate a ceiling still exists for those who have

Table 3.3. Career History Statistics by Salary Range.

Group	Salary Range	Total	Average Number of Jobs	Average Years in Present Job	Average Years in Fund Raising	Average Years per Job
All females	Under $39,999	419	2.28	2.87	6.04	2.86
	40,000–59,999	371	2.96	3.39	9.07	3.44
	60,000–79,999	104	3.67	3.76	11.86	3.78
	80,000–99,999	26	4.12	5.02	14.88	4.86
	100,000+	12	4.00	5.25	15.30	3.78
All males	Under $39,999	138	2.36	3.25	7.30	3.48
	40,000–59,999	287	4.83	4.06	10.85	4.20
	60,000–79,999	185	3.23	4.47	13.23	4.40
	80,000–99,999	91	3.63	4.41	16.47	4.73
	100,000+	63	4.35	7.35	20.69	5.33
Females with over ten years' experience	Under $39,999	81	3.33	4.99	13.09	4.99
	40,000–59,999	154	3.76	4.23	13.86	4.56
	60,000–79,999	60	4.27	3.70	14.45	3.94
	80,000–99,999	21	4.57	5.52	16.93	5.21
	100,000+	9	4.56	4.94	16.11	4.14

Females with under ten years' experience	Under $39,999	338	2.03	2.35	4.31	2.35
	40,000–59,999	218	2.40	2.77	5.57	2.65
	60,000–79,999	44	2.59	3.09	6.41	2.92
	80,000–99,999	5	2.20	2.90	6.30	3.37
	100,000+	1	2.00	1.00	8.00	8.00
Males with over ten years' experience	Under $39,999	37	3.30	5.64	15.45	6.42
	40,000–59,999	134	3.52	5.53	17.07	5.93
	60,000–79,999	112	3.93	5.05	17.62	5.27
	80,000–99,999	68	4.09	4.54	19.22	5.31
	100,000+	56	4.57	7.44	22.36	5.72
Males with under ten years' experience	Under $39,999	97	2.02	2.41	4.34	2.51
	40,000–59,999	148	2.20	2.62	5.21	2.78
	60,000–79,999	66	2.18	3.29	6.07	3.45
	80,000–99,999	18	1.94	3.94	6.08	3.86
	100,000+	6	2.00	2.42	5.08	2.57

switched jobs frequently. No one who reported having had 8 or more employers earns higher than $75,000" (p. 8).

Career Histories by Nonprofit Organizations

To determine if turnover among fund raisers differed by type of nonprofit organization, we analyzed career history data for all nonprofit areas. Table 3.4 presents career history information for all nonprofit areas for respondents with ten or more years and under ten years of experience in fund raising.

As indicated earlier, fund raisers with more experience tended to have more stable career histories than fund raisers with less experience. As Table 3.4 indicates, in each subsector, fund raisers with ten or more years' experience had more stable career histories (that is, more average years per job and more average years in present job) than fund raisers with under ten years' experience.

We combined fund raisers working in environment, public benefit, and religion into one group because of the small numbers in each subsector. Respondents constituting this group had the lowest average years per fund-raising job and highest average number of fund-raising jobs for both those with ten or more years' experience and for those with under ten years' experience in fund raising. Fund raisers in human service organizations with more than ten years' experience had slightly more stable career histories than fund raisers in other nonprofit subsectors.

Career Histories and Subsector Changes

Many fund raisers not only are concerned that some fund raisers change jobs too often but they also have a particular worry about fund raisers who move from one nonprofit subsector to another. Because commitment to the cause is believed to be necessary for raising money, moving from one subsector to another calls into question the credibility of some fund raisers. As one interviewee said, "There are fundamentally different constituencies for different subsectors and I don't believe it is possible to change hats so fast." Another interviewee said, "I'm confused by people who move around in the nonprofit area. What do they know about the values that drive decision making in the new environment? I want

Table 3.4. Career Histories by Nonprofit Subsector.

Subsector and Years' Experience	Number	Average Number of Jobs	Average Years in Present Job	Average Years in Fund Raising	Average Years per Job
Arts and Culture					
Ten or more	68	3.94	4.96	14.76	5.03
Under ten	120	2.37	2.50	5.14	2.62
Education					
Ten or more	376	3.89	4.79	15.99	5.00
Under ten	466	2.25	2.69	5.13	2.65
Environment, Public Benefit, and Religion					
Ten or more	10	4.90	4.45	14.90	4.95
Under ten	76	5.96	2.39	3.39	0.73
Health					
Ten or more	184	3.89	4.76	17.10	5.03
Under ten	214	2.10	2.73	5.05	2.78
Human Services					
Ten or more	79	3.61	5.87	16.06	5.97
Under ten	114	1.94	2.58	4.63	2.73
Other					
Ten or more	37	3.81	6.97	17.72	5.64
Under ten	28	2.21	2.36	4.84	2.63

subsector jumpers to articulate how they see the values transfer."
Interviewees in the study who had worked in more than one nonprofit area made the case that the basic know-how is easily trans-
ferrable if the fund raiser enters the new area with the willingness
to learn about the specific organization and its constituents and a
belief in the mission and values of the new area. Some believe
there is validity in commitment to the nonprofit sector as a whole
that supports cross-sector participation.

Table 3.5 shows the incidence of subsector change by nonprofit
subsector. Fund raisers in education were less likely to change subsectors than fund raisers in any other subsector. This is most likely
related to the fact that in general fund-raising offices in educational institutions are larger than in most other nonprofit organizations. Larger offices provide the most fund-raising jobs and the
most opportunities for advancement. As a result, it seems reasonable to conclude that many fund raisers in education would not
need to change subsectors to advance, while fund raisers in other
kinds of organizations might.

Male fund raisers currently working in health organizations had
the highest rate of change across subsectors. Half of all respondents
currently working in health had worked in other subsectors. This
factor may be related to the recent development of fund raising in
many hospitals, compared to the field's longevity in other nonprofit
areas. Also, fund raisers' salaries in health are higher than in the
other subsectors, which enables health care organizations to attract
successful persons from all the other subsectors.

Analysis of career history data indicated that men and women
who had not changed subsectors had more job stability than those
who had changed from one nonprofit area to another. As indicated in Table 3.6, the majority of respondents had not changed
subsectors and their average number of jobs were lower than those
who had changed subsectors. Their years in present job and average years per job were also higher than those who had changed
subsectors.

Job stability decreased as the number of subsector changes
increased. Both men and women with experience in four or more
subsectors had longer careers in fund raising than those in any other
group but they also had more jobs and lower average years per job.

Table 3.5. Subsector Change by Nonprofit Subsector.

Present Subsector	Total Number	Changed Subsectors		No Change	
		Number	Percent	Number	Percent
Arts and culture	104	42	40.4	62	59.6
Education	897	253	28.2	644	71.8
Health	442	220	49.8	222	50.2
Human services	218	83	38.1	135	61.9
Other	184	85	46.2	99	53.8

Table 3.6. Career Histories and Subsector Changes.

Group	Number of Subsector Changes	Number	Number of Fund-Raising Jobs	Years in Present Job	Total Years in Fund Raising	Average Years per Fund-Raising Job
All females	0	583	2.22	3.67	7.27	3.69
	1	203	3.31	3.19	9.73	3.04
	2	100	4.20	2.43	10.90	2.67
	3	39	4.97	2.05	11.63	2.36
All males	0	484	2.52	4.31	10.28	4.36
	1	166	3.37	3.81	13.60	4.16
	2	77	4.30	3.88	15.84	3.78
	3	35	5.97	3.91	20.23	3.49
Females with over ten years' experience	0	163	3.28	5.82	14.48	6.05
	1	92	3.93	4.17	14.04	3.95
	2	58	4.72	2.85	14.09	3.19
	3	24	5.13	2.40	13.94	2.77

Females with under ten years' experience					
0	420	1.81	2.82	4.43	2.77
1	107	2.77	2.25	6.02	2.33
2	42	3.48	1.83	6.49	1.93
3	15	4.71	1.40	7.44	1.60
Males with over ten years' experience					
0	208	3.40	6.21	17.56	6.28
1	102	3.73	4.90	18.22	5.33
2	58	4.40	4.54	18.62	4.43
3	32	6.16	4.17	21.38	3.63
Males with under ten years' experience					
0	276	1.85	2.85	4.67	2.91
1	64	2.81	2.06	6.12	2.29
2	19	4.00	1.75	6.86	1.80
3	3	4.00	1.17	8.00	2.00

This seems to indicate that people who are willing to make more radical changes also make more changes, but it could also mean that people who have worked in more than one sector have more value in the market, with more opportunities for advancement.

Summary of Career Histories

As we hope this chapter indicates, analyzing turnover and career histories in fund raising is a complex matter. To repeat, we think the data indicate that the high degree of turnover in fund raising is a result of the tremendous growth in the field and also that turnover rates will decrease as growth in the field levels off. There is ample evidence that the number of experienced fund raisers is increasing and that experienced fund raisers have more stable career histories. The data do not, of course, answer all the questions or fully explain the phenomenon of turnover in fund raising.

One particular set of questions requiring further study and thoughtful discussion concerns organizations that hire transients: Why do organizations hire fund raisers with transient career histories? Is it because of the scarcity of experienced practitioners? Do the persons doing the hiring in some organizations want the start-up expertise of transient fund raisers more than they want a fund-raising program characterized by a long-term commitment? Does the hiring of transients reflect the lack of real understanding about fund raising on the part of hiring administrators? Or does it reflect their conception of fund raisers as itinerant workers who go from organization to organization, harvesting campaigns, doing the essential work that no one else in the organization wants to do?

In the next chapter, we present additional information related to turnover and careers in fund raising, as we explore issues related to the decisions fund raisers make about their careers and their aspirations for the future.

Chapter Four

Attitudes, Motivations, and Career Decisions

In many occupations, people reach the highest levels of responsibility in the field by beginning in entry-level positions and steadily advancing up the ranks through a series of progressively more challenging assignments. Many consider this to be a model career history. It may not be the norm in fund raising, however, because most fund raisers have spent some time—and in some cases, significant periods of time—in other career fields. This chapter presents information from the survey on the factors influencing fund raisers' career decisions, their occupations before fund raising, and attitudes and motivations affecting their careers.

Snapshots

The following snapshots include one fund raiser with a career history that follows the model, two with unusual career experiences prior to entering fund raising, and two relative newcomers to the field.

A Model Fund-Raising Career History

Peter arrived in fund raising via brief early career experiences in the ministry, teaching, and student affairs, and eventually, in alumni relations at his undergraduate alma mater. In twenty years, he had had four progressively more responsible positions in fund raising at only three higher education institutions. At the time of this interview, he was forty-six years old. As vice president of development at a private comprehensive university, he earned more than $100,000 per year and was very much involved in family and community activities.

Peter entertained notions of various careers in his first two years of college, including law, computers, and business. The common feature of all these dreams, and of the others to follow, was the ambition to be at the top of the field, whatever it was. By the end of his sophomore year, Peter began to consider the ministry, and, after he graduated from college with a degree in sociology, he enrolled at a nearby seminary. After marriage and a few years in the seminary, he decided not to become a minister. A former associate invited him to become the assistant football coach at a high school. He accepted—beginning a practice that continues to this day; he has never applied for a job—and began earning a master's degree in higher education administration. He planned to work in student affairs—which, given Peter's inclination to seek the top of any field, meant becoming dean of students somewhere. Later, he was recruited for the position of defensive line coach and associate dean of students at a small college. Four years after graduating from college, he was again recruited, this time by the new vice president for development at his alma mater, for the position of director of alumni programs and the annual fund. Peter's reaction to this recruitment was:

> "No way. I will never get into fund raising." The vision I had was of a guy who wore polyester pants, a madras shirt, and white patent leather shoes and belt on the golf course. Asking people for money just seemed like a dirty profession. I thought you can't be a nice person and ask people for money, even though I believed that *giving* money was a good thing.

The vice president who introduced Peter to development became Peter's first important mentor in fund raising. He enlightened Peter about development by explaining that the function of fund raising was to help provide the critical resources a worthwhile institution needed to achieve institutional goals. Peter said he "really fell in love with development—and knew early on that I wanted someday to be a vice president for development." Four years later, the new president at a small church-related university in another state called to offer him the position of vice president of development. Although he had not been thinking about making a change, Peter was flattered and found the offer attractive. He accepted the job and stayed there for ten years.

He met the new president at his present university when he was asked to provide consultation in development. The president offered him a job. He was in the job for more than six years when this interview occurred. In the previous year, Peter had been recruited by search committees seeking to fill presidencies at four small private schools. Peter may decide to accept such a position one day. On the other hand, he was also considering the possibility of a vice presidency at a major private university, but consulting had its attractive points as well and may be the route he chooses some day.

Unlikely Fund Raiser

At the time of the interview, David was sixty years old, an Episcopalian priest who had been educated in exclusive private schools and universities. He had written two books, served as the rector of a parish, as a school chaplain, and as the headmaster of a prestigious private school. He had been the chief fund raiser for a Southeastern seminary for six years and was as far from the popular but unflattering stereotype of fund-raiser-as-used-car-salesman as it is possible to get. Distinguished, handsome, and scholarly, he was expressive, thoughtful, and self-disclosing during the interview. He was married and earned over $100,000 a year.

David graduated from a seminary that focused on preparing people for parish work, but he knew while still there that he wanted other opportunities as well. He remembered always wanting to be involved in some capacity that included both the ministry and education. He served as assistant pastor and pastor in local parishes for ten years and as chaplain and headmaster in private schools for twenty years. His career in development, though not part of his original plan, began when he was a headmaster and gained extensive experience in raising money. David believed that his seminary training and earlier professional experiences "were all very important as a basis for what I do now." David remembered how he first heard about his present job:

While I was on sabbatical as headmaster, the dean of this seminary called to ask if I would be interested in this job. It came out of the blue. He said, "I don't suppose you'd be interested in being director of development," as if to say, "No one, especially not somebody who has some credence, would really want to do this kind of work, would they?" I still don't understand that apologetic attitude many people have about development. My taking the job seemed very natural to me. I had background in development, plus I was a graduate of the institution, and a priest in this church. All of that is very useful in this job.

David talked about how his development job hooked his intellectual curiosity:

What is required is a real commitment to the mission of the organization and the ability to understand what is involved in order to help the organization to achieve its goals. It may not take a rocket scientist—and I wouldn't want to be one—but it is both enormously freeing and demanding. Although I was a pastor of a parish and headmaster of a school, I've never had a job where I am so much my own boss or responsible for planning my own time as is true here. This position is tremendously self-starting, much more than anything else that I have ever done. If I don't make something happen, it won't happen. That's very, very demanding and takes a lot of internal resources and intellectual horsepower.

David thought he could be at the seminary in the development position for another ten years but did not anticipate retiring: "I want my professional life to continue after I no longer work here. I write a great deal and I've published two books and I want to write more, but not full time. I would like to be involved either in helping people to develop professionally or in helping individual parishes raise money."

Unique Background for Fund Raising

Julia identified more with the organization she worked for than with the field of fund raising, but she was proud of her fund-raising expertise and success. She started her professional career as executive director of a small YWCA in Ohio, which, in an unusual way, led to a lucrative career in the modeling industry in New York City.

At the time of the interview, she earned about $48,000 per year in her position as the director of development for an organization that provides meal services for people with AIDS. She was bright, articulate, and gentle, with a sense of humor and deep spiritual values. Julia related that she began to learn the skills useful to fund raising while still in college:

> I always give my college sorority credit for teaching me techniques that come in very handy now, such as how to make things out of crepe paper and organize people. It's amazing how many times it has really been good to know how to make those flowers and how to use the "Tom Sawyer" technique to get the work done.

Julia became involved in presenting fashion shows for the Y membership, and through those activities, became involved in a volunteer capacity with a competition for aspiring models. The modeling firm that provided the prize for the competition offered her a clerical job in New York. That was the beginning of a seventeen-year career in the modeling business. Within nine years, she went from the position of receptionist to that of vice president of the firm. After a time, she decided to start her own business, which "took great courage because I was giving up the security of health insurance and retirement plans, and I did come from Ohio, after all."

Her company produced and presented a series of workshops and seminars for people who wanted to enter the modeling business. The business paid for itself but wasn't paying her enough so eventually she closed the business and was not sure what she wanted to do next. At that time, she had a friend who was dying of complications from AIDS and she became one of a team of people who helped to take care of him until he died eight months later. Julia noted:

> I was with my friend when he died. It was a mystical experience. So much happened in that moment and I didn't want to lose the gift that I had gotten from that experience. I wanted to talk about it and you know that you can clear a room in a second if you want to talk about death.

Julia found a support group for people to talk about death associated with AIDS. The person leading the support group was now her boss, who eventually offered Julia a job at the organization "to work on death education workshops, and a book about the organization, and some other things." About three months after Julia began the job, two things happened. The first was that the director of development left. The second was that the board of directors decided that death education was not a part of the mission, that "the mission was feeding homebound people with AIDS, period." Julia was asked to fill in temporarily in the development position. Although she had had no training and no specific preparation for development, she did have executive experience, and she "knew promotion because managing models is promotion."

One of the reasons the previous development officer left was because the organization was "having a tough time raising money." Raising money was a huge task because of the way fund-raising goals were set. In Julia's words:

> We don't estimate how much money we can raise and then set up a program. This organization has the commitment that no one will go without service. If you call and you qualify, you're fed. We don't care where you are or what we have to do to get the food to you. My job is to underwrite that. In the two years that I have been here, the fund-raising goal grew 40 percent one year and 30 percent the next. They tell me how much I need to raise and then I have to plan how to get that amount from our various funding streams.

Julia did not think the course of her career was particularly remarkable and also saw continuity in the professional steps she had taken:

> I brought a lot of social work thinking to the modeling business, which is why I was good at the modeling business, and I bring a lot of promotional thinking to fund raising, which is why I'm good at fund raising. My career in the modeling industry gave me self-confidence and the knowledge that there's not much I can't do if I break it down into little pieces and take it one day at a time. I really like to have my heart and my head both engaged in everything that I do. My heart and head were engaged in the modeling business because I enjoyed the people so much, and this job fully engages both. I really feel honored to be spending my time doing this.

Julia was not sure what the future might hold for her career.

I don't have a lot of personal ambition at this time. It's something that has fallen away along with a lot of other things that I had once. My ambition is for this organization, for the people I work with, and for us to have the resources to do what we want to do. I can't imagine what my next job will be but I don't think there's anything I couldn't do if my heart and head are engaged. If someday what I do here is not fun anymore, then I will find another way to use my time.

Uncertain About Fund Raising

Deborah was twenty-seven years old at the time of interview, single, and a college graduate with a degree in political science. She was petite, attractive, and articulate. She clearly knew the development business and her knowledge was all self-taught—she had never had a mentor in this field. Before accepting her first job in development, she worked for short periods as a nursery school teacher and for a market research firm. At the time of the interview, she worked as the director of development for a small private school in a large Southeastern city. Throughout her high school years, she had worked for this school as a camp counselor. She earned $25,000. Although the goals for the annual fund-raising program were modest, Deborah's fund-raising program was complex, involving an annual fund, major gifts, and planned gifts.

She started her first development job in 1988. One year later, the director of development left and she accepted the promotion to the position of director. Although pleased to be offered the job, she thought that the headmaster "realized that I was a real bargain. I was hired at about $16,500 and then my salary was increased to $23,000, which was a big jump but still very modest." After five years, Deborah said she liked some aspects of fund raising but she thought she was not "aggressive enough" and that she "would be petrified to go out and solicit a gift."

At the time of the interview, her school was starting a new campaign. She wanted to work on the campaign but thought that she would probably want to leave a year after the campaign ends. She might want to try something new then but did not know what it might be. Deborah noted, "Right now, I'm raising money for rich kids and earning very little salary myself." Herself a product of private schools, Deborah said:

> This is a great school and parents and alumni should support it, but there are so many other great places that need money more. I could see myself going into another nonprofit area, an organization that really needs the money, where I think I can be more committed in my heart to fund raising. But I know that those places don't pay good salaries. If I find that I do need more money, I don't know what I'll do.

She also did not think she would like working in development in a large organization because she did not want to specialize in just one aspect of fund raising (even though that is where she would have more opportunity for career advancement and high salary). She liked being involved in the whole program. She said that sometimes she thinks about selling residential real estate. She noted:

> That's hard work, but at this point it seems so much easier than what I'm doing here. There's a lot of stress in my job and I work long hours. There's a lot of pressure and stress, and their expectations of me are high. It is frustrating when I see that my friends are earning more money than I am. I see other people whose jobs aren't as stressful, who don't have as much responsibility, and they're getting paid more. If I'm going to stay at a very low salary level, I want to be more committed to the mission. I need to see that I'm doing something for somebody who really needs it as opposed to fund raising for a school for privileged children.

Committed to Fund Raising

Rosalie was just under thirty when this interview occurred, and she had already spent almost a decade in fund raising. She had been working for six years in health care development and at the time of the interview was days away from changing jobs. She had an undergraduate degree in psychology and was completing requirements for an MBA. After graduating from college, her original plan was to earn an MBA right away and work in human resources.

She said, "Of course, I hadn't thought about becoming a professional fund raiser, because no one goes through college thinking that."

As a volunteer for the alumni phonothon where she was an undergraduate, she found she "was really good at calling people and getting pledges. I really liked doing it. I would get a high, knowing I was helping the university." That volunteer position led to a two-year internship at the university, after which she began her first job in development for the health care organization she was about to leave. She started there as a campaign associate and staffed the employee campaign. She also worked as staff to volunteers and wrote proposals for grants. Eventually, she assumed management responsibility for annual giving. Although she knew she could still learn from her present boss, she also had begun to think she was ready for a position as chief development officer in a smaller hospital "if a good opportunity came up, which is exactly what happened." She was recruited by a search firm for a position in a hospital in another community and would start her new job in about two weeks.

Rosalie said she had been told that she had "what it takes to go all the way in this business and that's really been encouraging." She said she was "very pleased with the path" her career had taken so far, and that she was "farther along" than she thought she would be. She had met the requirements to earn certification from NSFRE and AHP and had reason to believe she was the youngest person to have earned each of those certifications. Her current salary was $55,000 and she was looking forward to a 24 percent increase—to $68,000—in her new job. Saying she now made "more money than I ever thought I would," she added:

> I know I have the potential to make a six-figure income in the
> next ten years. I love what I do and it's an interesting field. I'm
> really glad I found this field. I don't know how else I would have
> found it if it hadn't been for my alumni phone calling.

This talented young fund raiser found it difficult to speculate about what exactly she foresaw regarding the future of her career because of the complications of balancing a career with raising a family. However, she had been told that her new position eventually could evolve into a vice presidency to oversee the foundation and marketing and public relations, and she thought she might be interested in that. On the other hand, she also thought she might someday want to go to a larger organization with more potential because "there is limited fund-raising potential" at her new organization. Although full of confidence, she was also realistic. She said:

> I could see being ready for the position of chief development officer at a large organization in ten to fifteen years, but not before that. I have a lot of growing and maturing to do.

Career Decisions

When fund raisers talk about how they happened to end up in this field, someone—like Rosalie—usually points out that no one grows up dreaming about becoming a fund raiser. The majority of fund raisers enter the field after they have had experience in some other field. Many fund raisers say they got into fund raising "by accident" after they were involved in some aspect of program delivery or service provision, and, because they were committed to the organization or to the value of the mission, they became involved in fund raising to help provide the resources for the organization to continue its work. Often they will make reference to the management, communication, and relationship skills they were able to transfer to fund raising and the pleasure and satisfaction they found in fund-raising work. Few practicing fund raisers will say, "I thought fund raising would be a meaningful and rewarding career where I could make a difference so I prepared myself through formal education, internships, and professional seminars to enter the field."

Only 15 percent of all respondents (140 women and 128 men) reported having had no occupation other than fund raising as an adult or since college. Of the 145 respondents under the age of thirty, only 44, or 30 percent, had had no other occupation, indicating that even among the youngest people in the field, most have had previous occupations. Of the 198 respondents in their first or second year in fund raising, only 11, or 5.6 percent, had no former occupation, indicating that, even among those newest to the field, most had had previous occupations. Therefore, although fund raising may be one of the "25 Hottest Careers" in the country—at least according to the national magazine that approached the president of the NSFRE for information (Lewis, 1995)—and young people today are able to complete graduate degrees in nonprofit management and philanthropy, most people are still entering the field after working in some other occupation.

As indicated in the 1992 NSFRE membership survey report, "Ours is not a profession which is easily understood or entered into automatically. For the most part, individuals have to find out about it through venues other than upbringing or schooling [and] it is not a profession that appears to be attractive until a degree of social 'maturity' takes over" (Mongon, 1992, p. 4). Even when people deliberately seek employment in the nonprofit sector, they usually do not first enter the fund-raising field.

Occupations Before Fund Raising

Respondents were asked to list their occupations before entering fund raising; the 1,480 respondents who did so provided 2,659 total responses, meaning that many respondents listed more than one former occupation. Responses were summarized into occupational fields, as shown in Table 4.1, which indicates that respondents most often formerly worked in education, advertising and promotion, business, and the media.

Teaching of some form was the single most frequently reported former specific occupation for both men and women. Other occupations frequently reported by men included sales, higher education administration, nonprofit administration, public relations, the military, and marketing. Other occupations frequently reported by women included public relations, clerical, marketing, sales, nonprofit administration, and retail.

Among the eighty-two respondents interviewed for this study, sixty-eight had previous occupations before fund raising. Teaching was also the single most frequently reported former occupation among interviewees. One interviewee, indicating that he found that teaching had been excellent preparation for his career in fund raising, noted that he would not have been able to move directly from teaching into a profession such as law or the ministry and observed that the frequent movement between teaching and fund

Table 4.1. Former Occupational Areas.

Former Occupational Area	Total	Female	Male
Education	652	352	300
Advertising and promotion	338	235	103
General business	236	158	78
Media	180	125	55
Sales	164	72	92
Finance	144	65	79
Nonprofit management	130	73	57
Health administration or professions	119	86	33
Human services	99	66	33
Politics and government	77	45	32
Arts	73	54	19
Retail	67	42	25
Ministry	55	12	43
Sports	49	15	34
Military	46	4	42
Insurance	38	11	27
Law	35	14	21
Real estate	32	19	13
Hospitality	29	22	7
Human resource management	28	19	9
Systems and computers	19	14	5
Trades	18	7	11
Science and engineering	16	9	7
Parenting	6	6	0
Environment	5	2	3
Labor relations	4	1	3
Aviation	3	1	2
Foreign or international	3	0	3
Total	2,650	1,525	1,125

raising "probably reflects the lack of maturity and structure in each of those fields."

Reasons for Choosing Present Position

Respondents were asked to rate seven items using a scale of 5 (most important) to 1 (least important) to reflect the importance of the items in their choices of their present positions. Table 4.2 shows the mean responses for each item for all respondents.

As indicated, "More challenge or responsibility" and "Commitment to cause or organization" had overall average ratings of almost 4 on the scale. All other factors had overall average ratings of under 3. In general, fund raisers' ratings for more challenge, commitment, and pay are consistent with the values most interviewees expressed. Fund raisers are interested in advancement and are interested in working for organizations they respect. Although fund raisers are interested in making more money, this is not as important as more challenge in their jobs and commitment to the cause for which they work.

Organizational Commitment

As indicated in the previous chapter, it is generally accepted that long tenure of fund raisers is a factor in fund-raising success.

Table 4.2. Reasons for Choosing Present Position.

Reason	Female Mean	Male Mean	Total Mean
More challenge or responsibility	4.00	3.92	3.97
Commitment to cause or organization	3.64	3.65	3.65
Additional pay or benefits	2.93	2.97	2.95
Greater chance to reach fund-raising goals	2.66	2.84	2.74
Geographical location	2.63	2.62	2.63
Work with committed administration	2.56	2.70	2.62
Personal or family reasons	2.51	2.74	2.61

Note: Rating Scale = 5 (most important) to 1 (least important)

Because turnover in fund raising is higher than for some other nonprofit employee groups, questions often arise concerning the organizational commitment of fund raisers. Often, observers conclude that too many fund raisers lack sufficient organizational commitment, a conclusion that helps to keep negative stereotypes of fund raisers alive and healthy.

The concept of employee organizational commitment is of particular significance both to fund raisers and their critics. Organizational commitment has been extensively studied by psychologists and other social scientists interested in work and organizational behavior. In a much-cited study, Porter, Steers, and Mowday (1974) indicated that employees with strong organizational commitment have at least three attributes: a strong belief in and acceptance of organizational goals and values, the willingness to exert considerable effort on behalf of the organization, and a definite desire to stay with the organization. In general, other research (such as Lodahl and Kejner, 1965; Farrell and Rusbult, 1981; Porter, Steers, and Mowday, 1974; Morris and Steers, 1980; Meyer and others, 1989; Wiener and Gechman, 1977) is consistent in the finding that the organizational commitment of employees is more likely to be influenced by organizational or external conditions than by employees' personal values. Stevens, Beyer, and Trice (1978) suggested that factors with benefit and cost implications (which include economic and current job market conditions) are the most powerful influences on the organizational commitment of managers. Eisenberger and Huntington (1986) found that organizational commitment is strongly influenced by employees' perception of the organization's commitment to them. Eisenberger, Fasolo, and Davis-LaMastro (1990) found that employees whose general perception was that they were valued by the organization expressed more organizational commitment.

Of special importance is the frequent observation that there is no proven connection between organizational commitment and individual performance or organizational effectiveness. Several studies (Steers, 1977; Steers and Porter, 1979; Angle and Perry, 1981; Mowday, Porter, and Steers, 1982) indicated a weak relationship between organizational commitment and performance and suggested that organizations may behave in ways that retain the more security-minded—the employees for whom high performance is not important. Moderate or low performers may feel comfortable and committed in a nonthreatening environment while high performers seek challenge elsewhere. Organizations may end up with a more stable but less productive or creative workforce.

Individuals bring to their jobs multiple needs and desires, and the expectation that their work will make use of their abilities. The research indicates that when the organization provides an environment where these needs are met, employees are more likely to exhibit more commitment to the organization. Additionally, the research indicates that while personal characteristics, job characteristics, and work experiences all influence organizational commitment, work experiences—that is, the day-to-day experiences of working in a particular environment—most influence degree of organizational commitment. Nevertheless, most of the discussion in the literature about longevity of fund-raising staff treats the phenomenon of organizational commitment as more a factor related to the character of fund raisers than to employing organizations.

Both within and outside the field, many believe not only that fund raisers should be primarily motivated by organizational commitment but even that fund raisers should be expected to have higher levels of organizational commitment than other staff. No one ever mentions that fund raisers may require and expect more of their organizations than other staff, that is, that the overall quality of an organization may be more important to fund raisers than to some other staff. In other words, fund raisers may be more discerning and demanding employees than staff in some other areas. An organization is not automatically a good place to work just because the cause is a worthy one. Good fund raisers say it is too hard to raise money for organizations they do not respect, and it is hard for most employees to respect organizations that do not treat them with respect. Yet many fund raisers report frustration with how they are treated at some organizations and knowledgeable observers understand that turnover may reflect organizational problems and limitations as often as it reflects the ambitions and career concerns of fund raisers. (See further discussion of turnover and organizational commitment in Chapter Eight.)

Future Career Plans

In the present research, the survey asked respondents to indicate their present feelings about their future with their organizations and in fund raising for the next year, by indicating if they planned to stay with their present organizations and in the field of fund raising. These results are displayed in Table 4.3.

More respondents planned to change organizations than planned to leave the fund-raising field. As indicated, 68 percent planned to stay with their present organizations while about 80 percent planned to stay in fund raising in the next year. Because of the pressure to meet an increasingly challenging bottom line and the fatigue of constantly asking for money or depending on volunteers, many think of fund raising as a high-burnout career. However, these results suggest that burnout among respondents is minimal. More women than men planned to leave their organizations and the field of fund raising; these differences are probably related to the concentration of women in lower-level jobs where turnover is higher.

One survey respondent wrote that she thought asking fund raisers about their commitments and plans was useless because they would not tell the truth. We are not sure why this respondent thought that other survey respondents might want to disguise their intentions in a confidential survey, but we think it is part of a general sense many fund raisers themselves have that fund raisers are likely to be dishonest. Actually, our survey respondents predicted that they hoped to make more job changes than were likely to occur, based on studies that have reported turnover at 17.3 percent annually (Thomas, 1987, p. 6) and at 22 percent annually (Mooney, 1993, p. 16). Furthermore, given the fair amount of active recruiting going on in the field, there are a number of fund raisers who change jobs each year who were recruited when they had no plans to change jobs. A high number of our interviewees indicated that most of their job changes were the result of their being recruited when they were not seeking jobs. Future research should attempt to collect statistics on this issue.

To look at job stability compared to future plans, we analyzed career history data and data for plans related to staying at present

Table 4.3. Future with Organization and in Fund Raising for Next Year.

Plans	Total		Female		Male	
	Number	Percent	Number	Percent	Number	Percent
Future with Organization						
Looking now; plan to leave	442	25.6	255	27.9	187	23.8
No feelings either way	111	6.4	61	6.5	50	6.4
Plan to stay; never leave	1,175	68.0	626	66.5	549	69.8
Total	1,728		942		786	
Future with Fund Raising						
Looking now; plan to leave	191	11.0	124	13.1	67	8.5
No feelings either way	163	9.4	90	9.5	73	9.3
Plan to stay; never leave	1,378	79.6	730	77.3	648	82.2
Total	1,732		944		788	

organization and in fund raising. Table 4.4 indicates that those who planned to stay at their organizations had more stable career histories (more average years in present job and more average years per job) than had those who planned to leave. Similarly, those who planned to stay in fund raising had more stable career histories than those who planned to leave fund raising.

We combined responses for future with organization and future with fund raising. We found that 1,020 respondents (59 percent) planned to stay both in fund raising and with their present organizations, and 380 respondents (22 percent) planned to stay in fund raising but leave their present organizations, a number that is consistent with other reported studies on turnover in development. A total of 151 respondents (8.7 percent) planned to leave both their present organizations and the field of fund raising and 55 respondents (3.2 percent) planned to leave fund raising but stay with their present organizations. These results indicate to us that there is a core of fund raisers with significant commitment both to fund raising and their present organizations.

Table 4.5 shows information regarding fund raisers' future plans by subsector. As indicated, a total of 37.4 percent of fund raisers in arts and culture hoped to leave their present organizations, more than fund raisers in any subsector. There were no important differences regarding fund raisers' plans to leave the fund-raising field across different nonprofit subsectors.

Career Orientations of Fund Raisers

Gouldner's work (1957a, 1957b) was an early forerunner of studies in organizational commitment. He characterized professional or skilled employees as of two types, *cosmopolitans* and *locals*. He defined cosmopolitans as employees with low levels of organizational loyalty and high levels of commitment to specialized role skills and to peer groups outside the organization. He defined locals as employees with high levels of organizational commitment and low levels of commitment to outside peer groups and specialized role skills. Gouldner noted that organizations need both types of employees: cosmopolitans for their specialized role expertise, and locals for the stability they provide. Sheldon (1971) expanded the cosmopolitan-local dichotomy to include two additional types:

Table 4.4. Future Plans and Career Histories.

	Number	Percent	Average Number Jobs	Average Years Present Job	Average Years in Fund Raising	Average Years per Job
Future Plans with Organization						
Females						
Looking now; plan to leave	255	27.9	2.60	3.35	7.35	3.20
No feelings either way	61	6.5	2.70	2.60	7.90	2.90
Plan to stay; never leave	626	66.5	2.70	4.25	9.90	4.40
Males						
Looking now; plan to leave	187	23.8	2.95	3.95	10.70	3.95
No feelings either way	50	6.4	2.80	3.60	9.70	3.70
Plan to stay; never leave	549	69.8	3.05	5.35	14.30	5.20
Future Plans in Fund Raising						
Females						
Looking now; plan to leave	124	13.1	2.45	3.25	6.65	3.05
No feelings either way	90	9.5	2.10	3.50	6.50	3.50
Plan to stay; never leave	730	77.3	3.00	3.70	10.25	3.90
Males						
Looking now; plan to leave	67	8.5	2.40	3.70	7.40	3.60
No feelings either way	73	9.3	2.40	4.10	8.90	4.10
Plan to stay; never leave	648	82.2	3.25	4.65	14.00	4.00

Table 4.5. Future with Organization and Fund Raising by Nonprofit Subsector.

	Total	Look; Plan		No Feelings		Stay; Never Leave	
		Number	Percent	Number	Percent	Number	Percent
Future with Organization							
Arts and culture	91	34	37.4	7	7.7	50	54.9
Education	849	220	25.9	56	6.6	573	67.5
Health	414	92	22.2	21	5.1	301	72.7
Human services	201	56	27.9	17	8.5	128	63.7
Environment, public benefit, religion	83	22	26.5	5	6.0	56	67.5
Other	59	16	27.1	2	3.4	41	69.5
Total	1,697	440	25.9	108	6.4	1,149	67.7
Future with Fund Raising							
Arts and culture	93	13	14.0	10	10.8	70	75.3
Education	859	100	11.6	78	9.1	681	79.3
Health	415	42	10.1	29	7.0	344	82.9
Human services	202	21	10.4	26	12.9	155	76.7
Environment, public benefit, religion	59	5	8.5	7	11.9	47	79.7
Other	84	8	9.5	10	11.9	66	78.6
Total	1,712	189	11.0	160	9.3	1,363	79.6

local-cosmopolitans with high commitment to both their fields and their organizations and *indifferents* with low levels of commitment both to the field and the organization. Bloland and Bornstein (1991), whose work formed the basis for one aspect of the present study, used a similar typology specifically for fund raisers. The four career orientations they identified are as follows:

- *Professional.* Equal commitment to organization and field of fund raising.
- *Booster.* More commitment to organization than to field of fund raising.
- *Careerist.* More commitment to field of fund raising than to organization.
- *Placebound.* No commitment either to organization or to the field of fund raising. Our data indicate that this label may be a misnomer; we use the term *Indifferent* for the concept.

Bloland and Bornstein implied that the professional orientation was the ideal, but they also noted that this orientation is difficult to achieve in practice because loyalty to one side—the organization or the field—"tends to attenuate commitment to the other" (p. 106). Those with a professional orientation may be expected to act always in the best interest of their organizations, to be actively engaged in developing their own skills and knowledge in fund raising, and to act always in a manner that earns respect for and even increases understanding of the field. They may also be expected to play an active role in professional organizations, demonstrating their commitment to strengthening the field overall.

Boosters may be expected to act always in the best interest of their organizations and to be concerned about increasing their knowledge and skills in fund raising, but they are presumed to have less interest and concern for the overall image or strength of the field. They may be less likely to identify professionally with other fund raisers and may be less likely to take an active role in advancing the goals of fund raisers' professional organizations. Some boosters may attempt to differentiate themselves from other fund raisers, especially from those whose strongest professional identity is to the fund-raising field. One of the interviewees for this study said, "I don't think of myself as a fund raiser. I think of myself as a university administrator whose present assignment is in development." Fund raisers with professional and careerist orientations see this attitude as disrespectful to the field, believe it reflects contempt for the field, and is evidence of the deep and general discomfort, even among some who do it, about fund-raising work. Boosters may be less likely than professionals to remain in the field.

Careerists, whom Bloland and Bornstein said may be called "migrant workers" (p. 106), are a source of concern to professionals and boosters because these fund raisers do not appear to have sufficient organizational commitment. Fund raisers of this type are presumed to operate in ways to make themselves look good, without sufficient concern for the long-term interest of the organization. They tend to emphasize expertise in fund raising more than values or commitment to a mission or cause. These fund raisers may be skilled and competent. One interviewee related:

> I once had a boss who changed jobs every two years, adding $20,000 or more to his salary each time. He would stay long enough to use up his bag of tricks and look like the wonder kid. I don't disrespect him because these organizations were better off when he left. He was very good at what he could do in two or three years.

Another interviewee characterized one careerist of his acquaintance in this way:

> I know someone who was in seven organizations in nine years and was also doing ninety full days a year as a paid consultant. This person was constantly on the speaking circuit. He parlays one year of experience twenty times as twenty years experience.

Indifferents (Bloland and Bornstein's "placebound workers") lack commitment either to their organizations or to the field. They may be people who managed to get jobs in fund raising at organizations that were conveniently located for them. These people may be spouses of persons whose own careers keep them in a particular locale, or they may perceive their jobs not as careers but merely as ways of making a living. Fund raisers with all other orientations look upon indifferents with disdain.

Table 4.6 shows the career orientation of respondents. Relatively equal proportions of men and women identified themselves

Table 4.6. Career Orientations.

Orientation	Total		Female		Male	
	Number	Percent	Number	Percent	Number	Percent
Professional: equal commitment to organization and fund raising	910	52.1	495	51.8	417	52.5
Booster: more commitment to organization	516	29.5	304	31.8	212	26.7
Careerist: more commitment to fund raising	267	15.3	130	13.6	137	17.2
Indifferent: no commitment to organization or fund raising	26	1.5	14	1.5	12	1.5
No answer	29	1.7	12	1.3	17	2.1
Total	1,748	100.0	955	100.0	795	100.0

as professionals. Women were slightly more likely to be boosters and men were slightly more likely to be careerists.

Reflecting Bloland and Bornstein's observation that the ideal orientation of professional is difficult to achieve in practice, only 52 percent of all respondents identified themselves as having this orientation. Only 267 (15.3 percent) of all respondents identified themselves as careerists and only 25 (1.5 percent) as indifferents. In fairness to the careerists, however, it is possible that some of those who now are more committed to the field than to their organizations are potential professionals, that is, people who may move to organizations that capture more of their commitment.

We examined the career histories of those in each of the four career orientations. Table 4.7 shows the results of that analysis.

As indicated, indifferent females and males had the fewest total years in fund raising. Female and male careerists had a high number of total years' experience in the field and also more jobs in fund raising than professionals. They had been in their present jobs for a shorter time and had the highest number of jobs in fund raising. Female and male boosters each had the highest average number of years in present organization and the lowest average number of fund-raising jobs.

Table 4.8 presents information regarding fund raisers' present commitments by nonprofit subsector. As indicated, more than 50 percent of fund raisers from each nonprofit subsector (except for those combined in environment, public benefit, and religion) reported equal commitment to fund raising and to their organizations. Fewer than one-fourth of fund raisers from each nonprofit subsector reported more commitment to fund raising than to their organizations.

Fund Raisers' Attitudes and Motivations

The data in this chapter provide information about some of the attitudes and motivations fund raisers have regarding their work. The survey indicated that more than eight out of every ten fund raisers worked in some other field, such as education, business, or public relations, before entering fund raising, and that the opportunity for more challenge and responsibility were important in respondents' choices to accept their present positions.

Table 4.7. Career Orientations and Career Histories.

Orientation	Number	Percent	Average Number Jobs	Average Years Present Job	Average Years in Fund Raising	Average Years per Job
Females						
Professional	501	52.6	2.94	3.12	8.73	2.97
Booster	307	32.2	2.31	3.81	7.38	3.66
Careerist	131	13.7	3.30	3.04	9.00	3.04
Indifferent	14	1.5	2.75	2.67	7.25	2.52
Males						
Professional	422	53.9	3.08	4.23	12.94	4.46
Booster	219	28.0	2.53	4.24	9.79	3.53
Careerist	129	16.5	3.75	3.56	12.59	3.57
Indifferent	13	1.7	2.46	2.23	6.27	3.14

Table 4.8. Commitment to Organization and Fund Raising by Nonprofit Subsector.

Subsector	Total	Equal Commitment		More Commitment to Organization		More Commitment to Fund Raising		No Commitment	
		Number	Percent	Number	Percent	Number	Percent	Number	Percent
Arts and culture	91	48	52.7	29	31.9	14	15.4	0	0.0
Education	855	466	54.5	281	32.9	103	12.0	5	0.6
Environment, public benefit, religion	90	32	35.6	37	41.1	20	22.2	1	1.1
Health	415	243	58.6	98	23.6	69	16.6	5	1.2
Human services	204	105	51.5	72	35.5	26	12.7	1	0.5
Other	69	37	53.6	15	21.7	16	23.2	1	1.4
Total	1,724	931	54.0	532	30.9	248	14.4	13	0.8

As noted, research from other fields indicates that organizational commitment is more closely related to organizational or environmental conditions than to employees' personal characteristics. Such findings lead to the suggestion that fund raisers may be more interested in working for organizations of quality than some other staff because it is too difficult to raise money for an organization that a fund raiser cannot respect and believe in. The majority of respondents, however, indicated that they planned to stay with their present organizations and in the field of fund raising in the next year, with more respondents planning to change jobs within fund raising than those planning to leave fund raising. Those who planned to stay with their present organizations and in fund raising had more stable job histories than those planning to change organizations or to leave fund raising. This finding suggests that the majority of people working in the field are committed to their organizations and to the field of fund raising, and that those people in the field who have less stable career histories will make the most job changes. The implication here is one that experienced employers have long known—if you are looking for employees who will stay a reasonable length of time with your organization, look for employees whose track records indicate job stability in the past.

More than 50 percent of respondents indicated that they had equal commitment to their organizations and to the field of fund raising, and almost 30 percent indicated they had more commitment to their organizations than to the fund-raising field. Therefore, more than 80 percent of respondents had career orientations that were favorable to their organizations. Only 15 percent said they were more committed to the field than to their organizations and less than 2 percent said they had no commitment either to the field or their organizations. Taken together, these data do not support the perception of fund raisers as opportunists more interested in their personal aggrandizement than in the welfare of their organizations. However, this negative perception exists not only among those outside the field but among many fund raisers themselves. We will present an explanation for why the negative perceptions exist and why they prevail in Chapter Eight, when we discuss the challenges fund raisers face.

Chapter Five

Compensation Issues

This chapter presents data from the survey about the salaries of respondents. It also includes a discussion of some of the issues regarding the level of compensation in nonprofit organizations.

Snapshots

These snapshots reflect some interviewees' views on compensation and some examples of the issues regarding compensation.

A Simpler Lifestyle

Carl was fifty-seven at the time of the interview, had worked in fund raising for about four years, and earned about $50,000 per year as the director of development for a school in the health sciences at a major public university. Prior to entering the fund-raising field, Carl had worked for twenty-eight years in marketing positions in the banking industry. In the mid 1980s, he left banking to invest in the savings and loan business. In a short time, he had lost both his investment and his job. Deciding that "the banking business wasn't fun anymore," he began to consider other career options and fund raising seemed "like a natural place to look." Carl explained that for a number of years he had been in charge of the bank's charitable gifts, disbursing about $1 million in donations each year. He reviewed more than eight hundred requests for gifts per year. Additionally, he had served on the boards and helped raise money for several arts organizations. Furthermore, he indicated:

If you're in banking and are active in your church, you always become the finance chairman. I had been on the executive board of the Boy Scouts for years and went through some fund-raising campaigns with them. I knew fund raising as a corporate donor, as a volunteer board member, and as a church volunteer. I had always been fascinated with the process and with the people I met, so looking into fund raising for a career change was just a natural thing for me.

He learned of an opening for a development officer at a national agency and was selected for the position over other candidates because of his marketing experience. When he started in the position, he enrolled in NSFRE fund-raising courses, which he thought were well done and very helpful in providing a foundation in the "nuts and bolts" of fund raising. He found his first paid fund-raising job "very exciting," and added, "I don't think I have ever been as passionate about a job as I was about that one. I really got excited about what that organization was trying to do and how fund raising made it possible." Unfortunately, this noted organization endured a major scandal within the first year of Carl's employment there, and Carl's job was one of the many casualties as the organization first floundered and then regrouped.

Now, after over two years in his present position, he did not find the environment as exciting or the mission as compelling, but he continued to be intrigued by the way in which his marketing skills assisted him in raising money for the school. He noted, "I stayed in the banking business too long. I'm sorry I didn't get out and get into fund raising as a professional a long time ago."

Carl's career change and decision not to continue to pursue his career in banking had drastically reduced his family's income and dramatically changed his family in other ways. A few years before Carl left banking, his wife decided to return after an eighteen-year absence to the teaching career she had loved earlier. Now, their combined incomes equaled about half of what Carl had earned in banking. Yet Carl's only regret was that he had not gotten out of banking sooner.

After periods of sitting still and asking what is really important, I've come to realize that this is a good thing that happened to us. Economically, we've given up a lot of things. We no longer belong to the country club or drive fancy cars or do any of things we took for granted in our former lifestyle. But none of those things are important. Going to McDonald's for dinner is now a major event in my family's life and we really enjoy it now. Our lives are a whole lot simpler and we're all a lot closer because of it. We've had to make some serious adjustments in our lifestyle but it's worked out for the better. Working here is challenging and satisfying. It is certainly better for my health and state of mind and my family is happier, too.

As for the future, Carl thought he would stay in fund raising at the university, because he discovered that he enjoyed the environment of higher education. He thought he would earn a master's degree in psychology, something he had always wanted to do, and perhaps move into a broader management role in the university's development operation.

For the Money I Raise and the Money I Earn

Dan was the director of fund raising for a hospital consortium in a major city. He had worked in fund raising for ten years and was thirty-eight years old. He currently earned $87,000 and said he worked in fund raising both "for the money I raise and the money I earn." Dan had a master's degree in hospital administration, a field he originally chose because he wanted to combine a business career with helping people. Ten years ago, he was working in an entry-level position in hospital administration in another city when he learned that his alma mater was seeking to fill the position of alumni director. Dan got the job. He said:

They hired me for my administrative abilities, not because of my fund-raising abilities, because I didn't have any at that time. But they also saw that I was a people person and that really is my strong suit. I took the job because I wanted to get back to this area, and the $25,000 salary was a raise for me. I didn't know it at the time, but taking that job was the best thing I ever did, because it started my career in fund raising.

At the same university he eventually moved into the position of development director for the medical school. Dan said:

I was able to increase the annual fund from $250,000 to $300,000 the first year, to half a million in two years and to $700,000 in three years. It was just a great place, and it was good work, a lot of fun. The only problem was that they didn't want to pay me anything and by then I had two kids. We didn't have a house and wanted to buy one. I knew I was in trouble when the annual fund went to $700,000 and all they gave me was a $1,000 bonus. I kept trying to make it work there, but it didn't. I would have stayed at that job for the rest of my life because I loved it so much, but I couldn't afford to stay there. I had to provide for my family.

Dan noted that since he left that position, "They've had three directors and they're back to raising $250,000 a year, because they won't pay anybody to do the job." Five years ago he moved to his present job, one that also involved taking over a fund-raising effort "that was in trouble and in turmoil. Fund-raising revenues had decreased five years in a row before I came and, since I've been here, they've gone up every year."

From his own experiences, Dan thought that there were several problems for nonprofits related to compensation practices. He said:

In some places, they don't pay enough to get the job done. In other areas, the pay is excessive. Hospital administrators are making lots of money. The CEO of the top hospital here makes $800,000 a year. That's excessive, I think, even if he is running a $400-million business. I think what Aramony did was just awful and it hurt the United Way tremendously and hurt us all. If the salary of a corporate executive is a million dollars a year and an executive of an agency makes a couple hundred thousand dollars, I think that's reasonable and in line with what they have to do. Some people will say that's awful, but how do you get good people to do these things? See what you get when you hire someone for $27,000. See where it takes you.

Dan knew that people who did not work in the nonprofit sector, including potential donors, did not understand why some nonprofit jobs paid high salaries:

I have a good friend who won't give to the United Jewish Appeal because they pay people to raise money and all the donated money doesn't go to Israel. I told him that it costs money to raise money and if you want to attract good people to this business, you have to pay and provide benefits. I also told him that if he wants every penny he donates to go to Israel, he should spend his own money and take his check over there personally.

Dan planned to stay with the hospital consortium through the next campaign and thought that eventually he would be interested in a position as vice president for development in a large university or national agency.

Salary Is One of the Blessings

Greg, at forty-three, was the director of corporate and foundation gifts at a large hospital in a major city. He had been in the job for two years and earned $55,000. Early in the interview, Greg said, "It's very important for me to tell you that I believe that the Lord put me on this earth to do the work I do." Greg began his career at the YMCA.

> I grew up in the Y, and I always knew I would go to work at the Y after college. I worked at the Y every summer during high school and college. In college, every year I told myself that I would get a summer job where I could earn some decent money but every year I ended up going back to the Y because I loved kids so much. I loved helping the kids.

Greg worked at the Y for six summers and for sixteen years after that, at progressively responsible positions, ending up as the executive director of a YMCA in a smaller city near the major city where he now worked. He said, "From the beginning, I learned that at the Y your program lives or dies based on what happens in the annual fund campaign, so I have always been involved in raising money and working with volunteers."

Eventually, Greg said he began to realize that he enjoyed raising money more than he wanted to go on "running a bigger and better YMCA and worrying about whether the karate teacher was going to show up or whether we had a baby sitter lined up for ladies' exercise class." He left the Y and took a pay cut to accept a full-time fund-raising job with the Boy Scouts, where he worked for three years. Although he found the experience there valuable, he disliked the environment that he described as "a cutthroat situation, where competition and fighting over volunteers and who got credit for the gift was fierce." He left the Boy Scouts to take his present job, where much of his effort is directed toward providing behind-the-scenes support for the vice president of development and the hospital CEO. This role placed him in a very different kind of environment than the one he knew at the YMCA. He said:

> I was Mr. YMCA in the community. I was a big fish in a small pond there. Coming to work in the big city at this huge organization in a backstage role has been a real change for me and in some ways being out of the spotlight has been hard. But the good parts are that my phone doesn't ring at night with complaints from parents about the sports officials and I don't have to worry anymore about whether that bus filled with kids that took off this morning will return safely. I don't have any more of those churning stomach aches I had all the time worrying about other people's children. I don't work every weekend anymore, and I don't wake up at night worrying about this place.

Continuing to note the advantages of his present job, Greg added:

> I'm very happy doing what I'm doing. I am more than adequately compensated and the benefits here are great. I believe that the Lord calls on us and uses our gifts in many different ways. I've always felt that I had a responsibility to serve people and I know there is real worth and nobility in what I do now. Furthermore, because this job doesn't take up my whole life, I have more time to devote to my church, and because I make more money now, I can contribute more to my church. These are all great payoffs, blessings in my life. I don't do enough to deserve all the blessings I have.

Greg noted that he met very few people in fund raising "who are in the field simply to make a good living."

> Most of the fund raisers I've met, especially the good ones, are much more concerned with serving the organization than they are about their own incomes.

In regard to his own income, he said:

For the first time in my life I am being paid what I consider a handsome salary. I don't know if I am worth what I earn. I worked so long in the nonprofit world where I believed that I gave up high pay for the opportunity to do important work and I was happy to do that. Now sometimes my salary causes stress for me because I wonder if I really deserve it. So, on one hand, I really believe in the worth of the work I do here and, on the other hand, I wonder whether I am overpaid.

Regarding his future plans, Greg said:

Next month we kick off a $23 million campaign which will take four to five years to complete. I don't see myself going anywhere until that's over. Some day I think I might like to get into church fund raising. Every once in a while I'm tempted into thinking I would like to be the chief fund raiser for a major metropolitan YMCA but when I remember the live-or-die aspects of those campaigns, I lose my interest pretty quickly and start counting my blessings again. I don't feel the need to be the boss again.

Compensation in Nonprofit Organizations

Ironically, after decades of calls within the sector for nonprofits to become more businesslike in their management practices so as to increase effectiveness, efficiency, and accountability, there are now claims that many current problems facing the nonprofit sector are the result of nonprofits' success in making themselves function more like for-profit organizations. As Young (1983) predicted, the issues drawing the most fire are those related to spending practices by nonprofits. The spending practice most germane to the topic of this book is the compensation of nonprofit employees, which has been a subject of debate since 1992. In that year, the United Way of America forced president William Aramony to resign. His $463,000 annual salary drew harsh criticism in the publicity surrounding these events. Because the United Way is perceived by the public as primarily a fund-raising organization, the level of compensation of fund raisers also became part of the debate. However, as indicated in one of the snapshots presented earlier in this chapter, public discomfort with the notion that some people are paid to raise money did not originate with the controversy surrounding Aramony.

Nonprofit Salaries

It is generally well known that nonprofit employees earn less than employees in similar positions in the for-profit sector. For workers of similar skill levels, nonprofit salaries are on the average 5 percent to 20 percent lower than for-profit salaries and 11 percent lower than public sector salaries (Preston, 1989). The difference in earnings tends to increase with occupational level so that professionals and managers experience the largest wage losses— roughly about 20 percent less (p. 25) relative to their earning power. Generally, in the fields where for-profits and nonprofits directly compete (such as in day care and nursing homes), salaries are more comparable. In areas for which there is no counterpart in the private sector, such as philanthropy and religion, nonprofit organizations generally pay lower salaries relative to for-profit salaries for positions with comparable skills (p. 27). Overall, if the skills required for a position in a nonprofit organization are attractive to for-profit employers, the salaries of nonprofit employees in that position will be relatively high (p. 34).

Therefore, nonprofit employees who manage complex organizations or generate revenues are likely to be better compensated in the nonprofit sector than some other nonprofit employees, because these skills are highly prized in the for-profit sector. Nevertheless, the majority of nonprofit executives and fund raisers continue to earn modest salaries. Studies of the largest nonprofit organizations, which represent a small portion of the entire nonprofit sector, demonstrate that average salaries for some chief executives exceed $150,000 and average salaries for some chief fund raisers exceed $75,000 (Rocque, 1994). However, studies that include nonprofit organizations of various types and sizes report much lower average salaries for CEOs and chief fund raisers. For instance, one study (Millar and Moore, 1994) of 1,377 nonprofit organizations of various types and sizes reported median salaries for nonprofit chief executive officers at $53,850 and for directors of development at $42,000 (p. 38).

As indicated in Chapter Two, the major professional organizations for fund raisers regularly survey their memberships. These membership surveys provide an excellent historical record of the history of compensation practices for fund raisers. The CASE survey on fund raisers in education (Williams, 1996) found that during the five-year period 1990–1995, when inflation increased by 20 percent, average salaries in institutional advancement increased 26.9 percent, from $41,981 to $53,262. In the 1995 survey, the median salary for all respondents was $51,250; the average salary for someone with the title of vice president (the chief development officer) was $77,400. Of CASE members, 9.2 percent earned more than $90,000 and 49.5 percent earned under $50,000. The NSFRE survey (Mongon, 1995), which included fund raisers from all nonprofit areas, reported that the median salary for all respondents in 1995 was $46,100, up from $44,000 in 1992. In the 1995 survey, the average salary for someone with the title of vice president was $72,000. Of NSFRE members, 25 percent earned less than $34,000, 25 percent earned more than $64,000, and 5 percent earned $100,000 or more. These surveys indicate that the high incomes of nonprofit executives who make the headlines do not reflect reality for most nonprofit employees.

Following the Aramony Incident

There have been some notable developments resulting from the Aramony incident. Contrary to what some may have expected, salaries among the highest-paid in the nonprofit sector have not decreased. Gray and Greene (1995) reported that in spite of criticism and increased scrutiny, major nonprofit organizations have continued to pay top executives high salaries and to give increases and other benefits. Some officials also reported that since recent scandals have resulted in more attention to how nonprofits are managed, some boards have actually increased managers' salaries to elicit their best performance (p. 1). Although many nonprofit boards may indeed be taking a closer look at how they set compensation levels, few organizations reported reducing the salaries of top executives and some nonprofit executives received big raises (Moore, 1994). Speculations were that Aramony's salary came to represent the ceiling so that any lower amount was acceptable or that Aramony's salary made some nonprofit boards aware that their executives were underpaid. One prediction was that in the future nonprofit boards will consider providing forms of compensation other than salary, such as appointments to paid directorships, as a way to enhance overall compensation without drawing as much attention as a higher straight salary would.

A serious repercussion of the Aramony incident was the increased interest in nonprofit compensation on the part of Congress and other regulatory agencies. One U.S. congressman proposed a limit of $100,000 on all nonprofit salaries; others called for the increased enforcement of existing laws to force disclosure of salaries and other financial information (Goss and Moore, 1994, p. 1). Some of those who favor placing a cap on nonprofit salaries have pointed out that the president of the United States receives $200,000 in salary plus a $50,000 expense allowance, and a U.S. chief justice earns $124,000.

Most of the response from the nonprofit sector has been in support of current compensation practices. Many believe that high salaries are needed to attract the best managers and that the appropriate response to criticism is not to pay executives less but to explain and defend the need for salaries at those levels (Pomeranz, 1994). One nonprofit executive noted that "rewarding professional skill, entrepreneurship, vision, and leadership with high pay is not immoral" and "nobility of spirit combined with low pay is no assurance of quality" (Goldstein, 1993, p. 37). Others point out that overseeing hundreds of staff and serving as national spokespersons, labor negotiators, fund raisers, and fiscally responsible managers are demands that warrant handsome compensation. One nonprofit official indicated that the proposed $100,000 ceiling was too low and that trustees needed to be more vocal in explaining why nonprofit organizations have good reason to pay more than $100,000 (Greene and Moore, 1993). A university president stated that he thought university presidents are underpaid and that although he thought his salary of $304,000 was appropriate compared to that of other university presidents, it was still less than what he would earn in the private sector for a similarly responsible position (Leatherman, 1993). Those who disagree argue strongly that altruism should be part of the reason someone takes a job in the nonprofit sector and should be its own reward. As one nonprofit executive said, "The privilege of serving the public purpose ought to be considered part of the compensation package" (p. 37).

By law since 1987, the compensation of top nonprofit executives has been a matter of public record, but adherence to the law varies. Some officials support the law, believing that disclosure is important in controlling excessive salaries, while others are opposed to the law. One official opposing the law stated, "It is the responsibility of the board, in executing their ethical, legal, and fiduciary responsibilities to the organization, to judge the appropriateness of the compensation level for positions within the organization. Because you work for a charitable organization, you now have no right to privacy. This is one more straw on the camel's back that makes attracting the best and the brightest to the charitable community even more difficult" (Greene, 1992a, p. 24). One report indicated that the disclosure of top executive salaries threatens to "fuel the kinds of expressions of envy, interest, or outrage usually reserved for the compensation of ballplayers, legislators, or Fortune 500 corporate executives" (Greene, 1992b, p. 27). Some hope that salary disclosure will result "in a firm new demarcation of the boundary between for-profit and nonprofit and redouble efforts by board members to take an active role in overseeing financial and ethical performance of nonprofits" (p. 33).

Still others are troubled by the way controversy about high salaries for a very small proportion of nonprofit employees overshadows the more significant problem related to nonprofit compensation practices, which is that far too many nonprofit employees are undercompensated. Observing that nothing generates more discomfort and controversy than a discussion of salary levels at charitable organizations, Barbeito (1990) indicated that lower salaries and in some cases the lack of even minimum benefits for nonprofit workers reflect the failure of the nonprofit sector to apply its own values to its workers. Citing examples from her personal experience, Barbeito indicated that the prevalence of lower salaries in the nonprofit sector is often the result of prejudice and lack of information about nonprofits that prevail in the larger society. Her examples (pp. 40–41) included instances in which:

- Members of grassroots boards judged staff compensation by what they themselves earned and often resented paying staff more than they themselves made.
- A millionaire serving as a nonprofit executive believed that nonprofit employees should be willing to accept low salaries because they should be glad to sacrifice for the good of the cause.
- A business leader said that males (but not females) who chose to work for nonprofits were weak because they chose not to compete for higher salaries in the for-profit sector.

Van Til (1993) wrote, "Most nonprofits pay employees including executive staff at levels far below what is required to sustain a comfortable standard of living. While overcompensation is a problem of the visible few, undercompensation is the reality for the invisible many" (p. 14). He also noted that critics of high salaries for nonprofit executives usually do not address the disparity between executive and entry-level salaries, which he observed was a serious issue in itself because the "perception of elitism engendered by large pay gaps between executives and staff can only heighten doubts about the motives of nonprofit leaders" (p. 14).

Values and Nonprofit Salaries

It is obvious that both those who defend or criticize nonprofit salaries are discussing values, the same kinds of values that may influence a donor to withhold a gift because some portion of the gift will be applied to the cost of fund raising. In a capitalist economy, market conditions determine the level of salaries but other factors are influential as well. Bok (1993) observed, "The amounts people are paid . . . reflect our deepest values, motivations, and priorities. For better or worse, we can often learn more about what matters in this country by observing what we are willing to pay for than by studying the messages that come to us from pulpits and campaign hustings, lecture halls and editorial pages" (p. 5). Bok further noted that what individuals earn in various vocations influences the way in which talent is distributed in our society (p. 3). In his study of compensation practices over twenty years for six groups of highly educated professionals, he found that corporate executives' salaries doubled in real terms since 1972 while top federal officials' real earnings fell more than 25 percent (p. 65); and doctors' and lawyers' compensation rose while professors and teachers were no better off in 1992 than they were in 1972 (p. 65). He concluded that these disparities decrease the quality of some professions because more of the ablest young people choose to enter business, medicine, and law when society strongly needs better teachers, professors, and civil servants. In a related point, Bok also noted that the social, economic, and moral factors that influence salaries and create vast differences in compensation levels for various fields also serve to increase competition. Noting that competition is beneficial to society in some respects, it also creates the need to "ensure that everyone abides by the rules in a system that relies so heavily on self-interest and personal gain as the means to motivating people to work. . . . The more we inflate the rewards the more we tempt competitors to violate rules" (p. 262).

The snapshots that opened this chapter highlighted several aspects of the single most important conflict about compensation for fund raisers and other nonprofit employees: should they expect to be paid what their skills are worth in the for-profit marketplace or should they expect to be paid less, substituting the satisfaction of doing good for the missing income. This conflict reflects the pervasive question we identified in Chapter One about fund raisers— whether they should be skilled salespersons or impassioned missionaries.

Bok's observations that people of the highest ability are likely to follow the money and that widely disparate compensation levels across occupations influence quality serve at once both to complicate and clarify the discussion in relation to fund raisers. Because fund raisers are among the best-paid employees in the nonprofit sector, they draw criticism from within and without the sector, yet it is also probably true that some of the ablest people in the nonprofit sector will be those who have been able to compete successfully for the best of what the nonprofit sector offers. By extension, however, it is also clear that by increasing the financial rewards associated with fund-raising work, the field risks attracting those who may not have all the requisite and desired values and motives. As earlier sections indicate, opinions about compensation for fund raisers are value laden on both sides.

Present Research Results

In the rest of this chapter, we present numerical data from the survey on actual levels of compensation for fund raisers and qualitative data from the interviews revealing the opinions of some fund raisers on these issues.

Current Annual Salaries

The history of compensation for fund raisers has been well documented over the past ten years in membership surveys by professional organizations. Even though this information is available elsewhere, we included a question about compensation in our survey so as to be able to compare salary with other responses to our survey and interviews. In general, the results from our research reflect the same levels and patterns of compensation identified in membership surveys. Our survey asked respondents to indicate the range in which their present salaries fell. The ranges were $39,999 and under, $40,000 to $59,999, $60,000 to $79,999, $80,000 to $99,999, and $100,000 and above. We asked respondents to indicate the range of their salaries rather than to list actual salary to ensure the highest number of responses to this item. All but thirty-one respondents provided information about their present salaries. For future research, we recommend asking participants to indicate actual salary or using smaller ranges in order to obtain more precise information than was obtained in this study.

As indicated on Table 5.1, about 4 percent of respondents reported earning salaries of $100,000 or more, locating themselves at or over the arbitrary salary ceiling for nonprofit employees discussed by Congress and the Clinton administration in 1994.

A total of 11 percent of respondents earned salaries of $80,000 or above, compared to the average salary ($75,481) of the highest 10 percent of federal workers; the highest 10 percent of accountants ($69,743); and the highest 10 percent of advertising and marketing employees ($76,200) (Special Libraries Association, 1995, p. 18). Nevertheless, as indicated on the table, the majority of respondents earned less than $60,000. The largest group of respondents (662 or 37.9 percent) earned between $40,000 and $59,999, falling within the range of average salaries of $46,100 and $53,262

Table 5.1. Annual Salary Level for All Respondents and Males and Females.

Salary Range	Female		Male			Total	
	Number	Percent	Number	Percent	F-M Ratio	Number	Percent
Under $39,999	426	44.4	138	17.5	3.09	564	32.3
$40,000–$59,999	374	39.0	288	36.6	1.30	662	37.9
$60,000–$79,999	107	11.2	189	24.0	0.57	296	17.0
$80,000–$99,999	27	2.8	92	11.7	0.29	119	6.8
$100,000+	12	1.3	64	8.1	0.19	76	4.4
No salary listed	13	1.4	16	2.0	0.81	31	1.7
Total	959	100.0	787	100.0	1.22	1,748	100.0

reported in the most recent studies by NSFRE (Mongon, 1995) and CASE (Williams, 1996), respectively.

We also asked respondents to indicate if they had received bonuses in addition to salary in the past five years; only 13.4 percent of respondents indicated that they had received bonuses during that period. Whether respondents were male or female did not appear to be related to whether they received bonuses, but respondents who worked in health care were somewhat more likely to report bonuses than respondents in all other nonprofit subsectors. These findings are similar to those of another study that reported that 14 percent of the nonprofit organizations surveyed provided bonuses and that health care organizations were the most likely to provide bonuses (McIver, 1996, p. 25).

We compared salary levels with titles, educational level, seniority in fund raising, type of nonprofit organization, and gender, and, consistent with the latest NSFRE and CASE surveys, found variations in salary levels for all these factors. In short, people with more prestigious titles, higher levels of education, and more years of experience in the field tended to earn higher salaries. In addition, also consistent with other studies, our research indicated that fund raisers in education and health care tended to earn higher salaries than fund raisers in all other kinds of nonprofit organizations; and, finally, our research indicated that male fund raisers earned higher salaries than female fund raisers, even when education, age, and experience in the field were held constant.

As noted, the relationship between salary level and education demonstrated in our research replicates the findings in the CASE and NSFRE surveys on this issue. For fund raisers contemplating pursuing graduate degrees to enhance their career options, our study indicated that a graduate degree is a good investment. This is an interesting counterpoint to our discussion in Chapter Six on the issue of how fund raisers think others can best learn about fund raising. As we will indicate, only a small minority of respondents thought that formal education leading to a degree was an important vehicle for others to learn about fund raising—even though it appears that a graduate degree (as a credential, in contrast to its specific educational content) may be a qualification for higher-paying senior positions. Also, as we reported in Chapter Two, a higher percentage of those working in education and health care held graduate degrees than those in other subsectors. Mobility to higher-paying positions in these two subsectors especially may be dependent on graduate degrees, and fund raisers in these subsectors can expect to be compensated for their investment in their own education.

Gender Differences in Salary Levels

One of the most serious issues facing fund raisers in their efforts to increase professionalism in fund raising is the disparity in compensation for men and women. The fact of this disparity and its persistence have been documented from the earliest membership surveys completed by the professional organizations. The latest CASE survey reported that the gap in average pay for men and women was $13,000 (Williams, 1996, p. 14). The 1992 NSFRE survey reported that the gap in average pay for men and women was $12,000 (Mongon, 1992, p. 16).

As indicated in Table 5.1, our research found that as salary levels increase, the disparity between men and women also increases. The ratio of female respondents to male respondents for this item is 1.22, meaning there were 1.22 female respondents for every male respondent. If the proportion of women and men in each salary range were equal, the ratio would be 1.22. If the ratio for a salary level is more than 1.22, women are overrepresented at that salary level; if the ratio is less than 1.22, women are underrepresented. The ratio of women to men was 3.09 at the lowest salary ranges, indicating that women are greatly overrepresented in this range, while the ratios of women to men in the three highest salary ranges indicate that women are greatly underrepresented at these higher ranges.

While the two lowest salary ranges may include high numbers of women who entered the profession more recently, seniority does not entirely explain the difference in salaries. At every level of experience in the field, the average salaries for women in our study were lower than those for men, and women at every age range reported earning less than men, except at the lowest age range. It appears that some ghetto effect is indeed at work with women taking longer than men to get to the higher-paying positions and with fewer women getting there.

Both women and men reported higher levels of compensation for higher levels of education. Based on our data, there seem to be two separate and distinct compensation systems for fund raisers; one for women and one for men. The salaries of men were higher at every educational level.

There may also be a ghetto effect in the distribution of men and women among nonprofit subsectors, with more men in the higher-paying education and health care subsectors. When women do find places in education fund raising, they are "clustered over-whelmingly in independent schools as well as two-year colleges" where pay and status are lower (Williams, 1996, p. 15).

Even when they have the same qualifications in education, ex-perience, and age, women are likely to be paid less than men about 40 percent of the time. Our data yielded 127 pairs of men and women matched for education, experience, and age. For 52 pairs, or 40.9 percent of the cases, men reported a higher salary level than women of the same age, education, and experience. For 62 pairs, or 48.7 percent of the cases, men and women were paid at the same level. For only 13 pairs, or 10.2 percent of the cases, women were paid at a higher level than men with similar qualifications.

Conry (1991) noted parallels between fund raising and other fields, such as teaching, library science, pharmacy, and public re-lations, that have become *feminized,* that is, have changed from being predominantly male to predominantly female. When a field is feminized and the work is perceived as women's work, the lower salaries paid to women become the norm and organizations then have an available workforce that supplies cheaper labor with no loss in the effectiveness formerly obtained from higher-paid male staffs (p. 147). Noting that in fund raising and other fields under-going feminization, men dominate in higher-paying positions be-cause women start at the bottom and move to the middle while men start at the middle and move to the top, Conry further noted that in fund raising there has been "limited progress in two decades of change" (p. 151) on this issue. She called for more co-operation among professional organizations to monitor and study the problem.

Interviewees' Reactions to Compensation Issues

As a group, interviewees reflected widespread ambivalence and heavily value-laden opinions regarding compensation. More than half of our interviewees referred to compensation as an area of concern. Some believed salaries are too high; others believed they are too low. As already noted, some people left jobs to earn more money and some people took pay cuts to accept certain jobs. Some were concerned that some salaries for fund raisers and nonprofit CEOs have become so high that they are eroding public confidence and trust in nonprofits. The following quotes illustrate some observations:

- "You don't go into a nonprofit to get rich. That was something I learned and accepted."
- "I think nonprofit executives are paid too much. I think I am paid too much, but I'm not going to ask for a pay cut."
- "How can you pay your CEO a quarter of a million dollars and ask for private support?"
- "High salaries make it look as if people are only in it for the money, which makes the whole field suspect."
- "I would find it hard to accept a six-figure income in my present job, but I would not feel bad about it if I were fund raising at Harvard."

Many interviewees thought that it was both fair and essential to the quality of staff in nonprofit organizations for nonprofits to pay salaries competitive with the other sectors. One interviewee noted:

> I think people in nonprofits are willing to work for less because of the satisfaction of the work. This sounds good but it is not okay because it doesn't attract the highest caliber, most qualified people. Also, I was treated with less respect by the business community when I was a director of development, dressed in the same suit I wore as a consultant, because they knew I didn't make as much money.

This interviewee appeared to echo the remarks of the business leader reported earlier who implied that people who are willing to forego higher salary for the benefits of working in the nonprofit sector are somehow inferior to those who would choose the higher salary. One interviewee said:

> In the nonprofit sector ultimately the salaries we draw limit the organization's ability to serve the people it exists for. If you want more

personal remuneration, by God, go work in the for-profit sector. There are lots of opportunities for people who have the skills Aramony did, the skills it takes to earn more than $500,000 per year, in the corporate sector. There are also people in the non-profit sector who have the skills that Aramony had who are willing to accept less than what they can make in the corporate sector. While Aramony did a great job for the United Way before he almost destroyed it, I'm not sure that his $400,000-plus salary was worth it. I don't know what Ellen Chao [Aramony's successor at the United Way of America] earns, but maybe the best thing that could come out of this is that a minority female heads up an organization in big trouble at a whole lot less pay and does it well.

Other interviewees said:

- "We should use good business concepts to run nonprofit organizations and that means paying good salaries."
- "We don't have good coherent arguments to make about why the director of a major nonprofit isn't overpaid at $250,000. Being entrusted to manage a multimillion dollar enterprise requires skills that are very competitive in the marketplace. It's as simple as that."
- "The problem is the press which is written for people who make the median income. Whatever the median is, if you're in the nonprofit sector and you make $1,000 more than that, the press will say you're a crook. Ball players making $4 million a year are an insult to the highly educated, highly dedicated, highly skilled people who work their fingers to the bone in the nonprofit sector and provide more value to society. The field has to become better at dealing with these issues."
- "Everybody only has a limited number of hours in the day. What does any one person do that makes them worth over $400,000? Did Aramony really work that hard?"
- "Like football coaches, good development people can now name their own price."
- "Although there is a strong religious underpinning to philanthropy, it is a tremendous leap to say that philanthropy and religion are the same thing and that people should have to take a vow of poverty to work in philanthropy. We live in a secular world and to get people to work a sixty-hour workweek

and take on massive responsibilities, we have to provide appropriate compensation."

One interviewee who came into fund raising in a highly compensated position reported that he had made a number of rapid career moves to earn more money before he came into fund raising. He said later in the interview that he advised people in fund raising to resist changing jobs for salary increases. He said he was not only concerned about the impact of turnover on the entire fund-raising field, but he also thought that "people need to understand that you can be happier with earning less and appreciate other kinds of rewards."

Undergirding the compensation issue is the ethic and value of the profession—what we have identified as the pervasive question about whether fund raisers should be missionaries or salespeople. For some fund raisers, the commitment to mission is a key motivation for what they do and many fund raisers are skeptical of those who become fund raisers because fund raising is a good career. Related comments:

- "Money taints virtue, money taints motivation, and as we pay people more, we're going to have people in the sector who are there for perhaps different motivations, but that doesn't mean we shouldn't pay people appropriately."
- "As salaries go up, there will be more career-oriented people in fund raising rather than those truly interested in the cause."

Regarding gender differences in pay, a number of interviewees thought that sexism in organizations was the reason for pay disparity, and some of them were not particularly concerned about this. One interviewee, a senior executive in her organization, treated it as a matter of fact that there was gender pay disparity at her own organization. Ironically, the mission of her organization was to serve women and help them to advance economically and educationally. Others blamed women for accepting lower salaries, as one interviewee noted:

The pay disparity exists because women are willing to take low pay rather than no pay as they turn from being volunteers and because women are afraid if they say no to a low offer it will be accepted by some other woman. Women do not know how to negotiate well. Women are willing to take lesser salaries at all different levels. This is not all men's fault.

Regarding the concern that the field of fund raising could become feminized causing men to leave the field and salaries to drop even further, one interviewee said:

My biggest concern is how to keep men in the field. Women will not like it if this becomes an all-woman field. Forget about what the men feel. Women will not like it at all and it will not therefore attract good women because women won't come into the field either. In many other fields, the question is "How do we attract women and minorities?" The question for us is, "How do we attract more men and minorities?" The newcomers are 80 percent women and, in my opinion, the men among the newcomers do not distinguish themselves.

Another interviewee said:

One of the problems with this field is that organizations are looking at the costs of fund raising and not the benefits. Therefore, organizations think the answer is to hire young females because they can get them cheaper. The precipitous change in the field from the old-school, hail-fellow-well-met alcoholic boys to twenty-four-year-old underpaid females with no fund-raising experience is not right.

The ethical codes the American Association of Fund Raising Counsel (AAFRC), AHP, CASE, and NSFRE restrict members from accepting commissions based on funds raised. In general, our interviewees supported that restriction. One interviewee noted:

Commissions are stupid. A commission will absolutely disrupt a relationship with a donor. People will without question move donors faster. They will move donors illogically, irrationally, in pursuit of commissions.

Although the codes of ethics mentioned here do not allow for such, one interviewee thought that paying fund raisers a percentage of funds raised was acceptable in organizations with limited budgets or in start-up phases. There is some public sentiment in support of this notion.

There was broader support among interviewees for use of bonuses to reward fund raisers for good work. The NSFRE code of ethics allows for bonus pay as long as bonus pay is available to all employees in the organization. However, as we reported, we did not find wide use of bonus pay. Interviewees generally thought that if bonuses were available, they should not be based only on fundraising totals. Interviewees suggested using multiple measures in addition to total dollars raised to take effort and circumstances into account and to ensure that the expectation of a bonus would not undermine ethics and the highest standards of practice. One interviewee said:

> Some places are paying bonuses to individuals for productivity or for going over goal. I have a real problem with that because fund raising involves so much team effort, and awarding bonuses to individuals can encourage dishonesty. Furthermore, what about gifts that come in from estates that no one knew anything about? Who gets bonuses for those gifts? I think it is usually trustees coming out of a corporate environment who are encouraging bonuses for performance, and we need to be stronger about resisting some of those attempts.

We will return to the issues surrounding compensation again in Chapter Eight, when we discuss the critical issues, challenges, and rewards facing fund raisers.

Chapter Six

Learning About Fund Raising and Improving Practice

This chapter presents information about how people working in the field learned the craft of fund raising and how they think other people coming into the field should learn. The chapter also includes information on respondents' ideas for improving the practice of fund raising and on their concerns regarding ethical fund raising.

Snapshots

The following snapshots present examples of fund raisers who came into the field as mature people who had worked in other fields. The snapshots describe why these fund raisers came to work in fund raising, how their previous experiences were useful to them, and how they felt about fund raising. In each case, the motivation to work as fund raisers and to be effective in their work comes from deeply personal commitments, values, and beliefs.

From College Presidency to Fund Raising

At sixty-three, Harry was executive director of development at a midsized public university in a Midwestern town. He had a doctorate in higher education, had been a college president, and currently earned about $70,000. As an undergraduate, he majored in theology and psychology. After graduation from a small church-related college, he was asked to fill in there for one year in the position of dean of men. The president eventually appointed him permanently to the position. After graduate work in student affairs, he was named dean of students at the same college, and, after completing his doctorate, he became dean of students at a much larger public university. Several years later, he was invited to apply for the position of president at his alma mater; he was selected for the position, served for eight years, and, among other things, learned how to raise money.

In his last year there, he began to think that he had done all he could as president. He explained:

> I took over an institution that had not done well financially in the years prior to my presidency. It took several years, but we wiped out the operating deficit, and we also made good progress on the capital debt. Some of the budget-tightening actions I had to take had negative effects on some of my relationships at the college. When you have to let people go in a small, close-knit community it causes negative reactions. Although they didn't run me out of town, I knew that some hard feelings had built up, and I realized that it was time for me to step aside.

Harry resigned, thinking that he would become president at another institution, but, he said, "That didn't happen. I was a finalist at three institutions but was not selected."

He was offered a development position at a prestigious private college in another state, which he turned down because he decided not to relocate his family while his youngest daughter was still in high school. Instead, he accepted a position with a publishing firm and reflected on his career. He was pleased about what he had been able to accomplish as president of his alma mater and disappointed that he had not accomplished more. He was also disappointed that his search for another presidency was not successful, but he was pleased about the enthusiasm he was able to generate at the private college where he was offered a development position. As more time passed, he realized that he had genuinely enjoyed the fund-raising part of his work as a president and was confident of his ability to be effective in that role. Although he recognized the serious responsibilities associated with fund raising, he began to think that a fund-raising position might be as challenging and rewarding as a presidency without as many burdens.

When his family was ready to relocate, he was able to throw himself wholeheartedly into the search for a development position in an institution he could "care deeply about" and where he could be helpful. He found his present position, had been there for seven years, and was satisfied that he had taken the right course. He said:

> The best part about fund raising is the opportunity to work with people who want to do something meaningful with their money. My only regret is that I wish I had been able to interest more wealthy people in my alma mater. I enrolled at that college the year it was founded and eventually became president there, so I have a lot of emotion about that institution. I would love to see it become more secure. Fortunately, they're doing better in the last two years. Our youngest daughter is on the staff there now. She serves as coordinator of alumni relations and special events. When I retire, we'll return to that area.

Harry plans to retire in two years. Of the environment and the immediate future, he says:

> Fund raising is getting tougher because there are so many more organizations out there competing for dollars and many of them are playing hardball. My biggest dream is to get a commitment for one more endowed chair for this institution. I'd love to be able to plop that on the president's desk before I leave. It will take everything I have to accomplish that, if it is even possible. Right now I don't see the prospect on the immediate horizon, but I'm not going to forget about it. I would love to be able to do that before I hang it up.

The most enduring satisfaction Harry had about his work was in knowing that the results of his work would continue to benefit the university long after he had gone. He explained:

> I have a sense of pride about the new buildings on campus that I've worked to help build. It feels good knowing they'll be here for a long time. I'm also leaving in the files a study of the family histories of some of our prominent families. I constructed these histories so I could talk with them intelligently about their families. That's been rewarding to do and should be helpful to the staff after I'm gone.

He also felt very gratified by the relationships he had developed with donors.

> [Some donors] actually come to my door because they want to talk to me. I don't know if it is because of my undergraduate background in theology, but I have been able to provide a listening ear in relation to some of their personal problems. That also feels good—to know that I don't just take their money but give them something back.

From Banking to Fund Raising

Sandra, at fifty, was vice president for campaigns for the United Way in a large city. She had worked in fund raising for six years and earned a salary in the mid $50,000s. She said:

> Church and religion were very central values in my family life. I was very active in church as a young child. Many of the communication and interpersonal skills that I use today that people sometimes think I acquired through formal education were skills that I learned in Sunday school and other church activities. I remember these marvelous old church sisters who used to tell us that we were God's sunbeams, and we had to shine and talk to people so they could see God's light in us. One of these women was my Sunday school teacher and the only black woman I knew all through school who had a college degree. I never had a black teacher, so she was a role model for me. She had a degree and she worked downtown.

When Sandra was in high school, a teacher asked her if she was going on to college. She said her plan was to get a secretarial job downtown. She explained:

> If you were a young black girl and your parents were of the modest means that mine were, you wouldn't impose upon them the great task of paying for a college education. I was never given counsel that I could seek a college education by any other means. The best thing I could do for my parents and for myself was to become self-sufficient. So, I was going to seek a secretarial job downtown and be delighted if I got that. That teacher said I would never be happy unless I went to college because I would not get the chance to do

the things I could do without the degree. I didn't remember that until years later.

Sandra did get her downtown job. She worked as a medical secretary until her children came along and returned to that same job after her children were in school. "There was just no talent involved in doing that job," Sandra said. "I couldn't take any pride in doing it, and I wasn't happy there, so I began thinking about doing something else." Sandra decided to attend college but since she was "into being Super-mom at home," she enrolled at a college with a weekend program. She finished her degree in about five years, while she also worked full time to pay expenses. After graduation, she went to work in trust and estate administration at a large bank and believed she had a future in banking.

She did not consider a career in the nonprofit sector at that time, even though what she recalled liking most about the work was that it involved strong interpersonal skills and she liked being able to be helpful with something that most people found distressing. However, she soon learned that to move ahead in that department she would need a law degree and was not disposed to return to school at that time. As a way to buy some time to think about what to do, she volunteered to be the bank's loaned representative to the United Way. In her first week at the United Way, she began to think she might like to work there. She described as an "exquisite experience" her first-hand discovery that major corporations demonstrated their interest in the community and invested in the community by providing money, staff, and other resources to the United Way. She said:

> I grew up thinking that these corporations had been exploitative and also had denied opportunity to so many people like me. Learning that these organizations really do see that they owe something to the community was a profound experience.

Observing that many United Way staff are recruited from the ranks of loaned representatives, Sandra said that her skills in interpersonal relationships, communication, and promotion were not so different from those of other loaned representatives, but her enthusiasm for the work probably caused her to stand out in her group. She said:

> When I arrived here, I just never shut my mouth about how we could do this or we could do that and pretty soon people said, "Well, do it then," so I did. Then, they started to say that they would have to find a way to keep me.

Before her stint as a loaned representative ended, they offered her the job of running the volunteer training program and the management of the fund-raising division. She said:

> I knew I had a lot to learn but I believed that I had the heart for it. I thought I would feel good about working here but I went through wrenching soul-searching about what I might be giving up at the bank and what effect it would have on my family. Now that my children have graduated college and our house is almost paid for, I guess I can relax and know that I made the right decision. This is very important work, it's a dramatically dynamic environment, and I love it. I made the right choice.

She was promoted to the level of vice president two years later and currently was responsible for managing a staff of eleven people who conduct workplace campaigns.

Although she loved her work, Sandra sometimes still felt frustrated and restless. She said:

> I have this image from *Alice In Wonderland*. When Alice eats the mushroom, she grows larger and larger, and she doesn't fit in the room and her feet are kicking the door out. Some days I feel like that. There are many more things I know I can do, but I'm constrained either because it's not my shop or because there is no time.

Perhaps more so than in any other interview, asking Sandra what she thought she might do in the future opened up a flood of feelings. She said:

> I think about what I ought to do all the time. I am at an age where I have to decide if I want to start another career or move my career

to another level because either of those decisions would probably mean that I will not retire before sixty-five. If I continue to work until age sixty-five, then that means that I won't do all the volunteer things I always thought I would do after my children were grown. The more my professional responsibilities have increased, the less time I have to volunteer, so I no longer do the things I did that gave me great joy and that had some benefit for others. The more distance I get from that, the guiltier I feel about it. I always think I should be doing more.

Sandra said that if she were to leave the United Way, she would probably be most attracted to organizations providing services to young people. She added:

Seeing children in need of so many basic things and remembering where I've come from is incredibly humbling. I always think about young black people who are not going to have the same opportunities that my kids had. Sometimes I tell myself that nothing is more important than investing in young people and I ask myself at what point do I put all personal needs aside and go do that? Shouldn't I be doing more? How do I make time to do more?

In spite of her dilemma about where she might best contribute, Sandra's zest for fund raising was evident:

We have to help many volunteers through their discomfort about fund raising because it feels like begging to them. Or we have to deal with the discomfort many feel about asking for money to fund services. In some other fund-raising efforts, there is some tangible evidence for donors that they did a good thing. When you invest in the United Way, sometimes you're investing in people who go back on drugs, who commit a crime again, who don't become un-poor or who continue to have problems with their kids. Sometimes people have the perception that this is not a good investment. It is often a pleasant shock for them to meet actual people or learn of situations that confront that perception, as it was for me to learn about the commitment to the community that many corporations feel. The most exciting thing of all is to see the light bulb go on for someone. That's a moving experience for the individual when that happens. For me, as a fund raiser, it's a great moment because it means I just got a prospect for a larger investment in the future.

From Marketing to Fund Raising

Irene was the stewardship and financial development officer in the office of a large diocese of the Catholic church. At forty-eight, she was just completing her first year in this job and her first year as a paid fund raiser. She earned about $45,000 annually. A lifelong member of the church, Irene had worked in marketing for retail firms and had extensive fund-raising experience as a volunteer. Her job was a new position that the bishop had invited her to consider. The bishop was not very precise when he originally defined the new position, except that she knew she would be expected to undertake a "whole reevaluation of how the diocese raises money and to assist in the development of a long-range financial plan." The bishop explained that he had interviewed several people with professional fund-raising experience, but he thought that her knowledge of the diocese and her commitment to the church would make her more valuable in the position than would professional fund-raising experience.

Irene accepted the job, even though at first she said she was "just terrified." She concentrated on the many parallels between the new job and her former professional and volunteer experiences; her husband helped by telling her that she was just moving from "marketing for people who thought they were God to marketing for God." Supported by others' confidence in her, her commitment to the church, and the opportunity to work for the church, she tackled the job by starting out to learn as much as she could about the diocese's multiple constituencies and by joining a professional organization.

As she began to learn about the diocese and the great diversity of the parish constituencies, she began to feel more comfortable about how her volunteer fund-raising skills and marketing experience would help her to provide resources and direction for them in their stewardship programs. Irene said that the stewardship concept "looks like fund raising but actually it has a very different tone to it." She explained that each of the parishes was self-governed and they supported themselves through their annual stewardship campaigns in which members of the congregation pledged what they intended to give in the following year. She added:

Very few people know what other people pledge. We're very quiet about it because how much people give is between them and God. It is a very spiritual matter, very much a question of where people are in their spiritual journey. The people who give the highest percents of their income are people for whom the church and God are central.

While her orientation to the diocese's parishes increased her confidence, at the same time, she found that her experiences at professional meetings and workshops and conversations with other fund raisers were less and less helpful. She explained:

At these meetings there's a certain piranha tendency that I don't find very attractive. When I go to those meetings it's honestly torture for me. I have a very hard time. People say, "What's your annual fund goal? You have to have a goal." At first, I thought, "I'm not doing anything right." Now, I just find it offensive, because so many fund raisers operate within a framework, a formula, and their attitude is that that's the only way to do it, and they're really aggressive about it. I had to evaluate if the recipe would work for us, and at this point in my stewardship program the answer is, one recipe doesn't work. We're not all one size. One size does not fit all. [It's important to] respect the culture of different congregations. Some congregations approach their giving in a fundamentalist way. They'll challenge people to give a certain amount. That would never happen in some other congregations. Some parishes use what we call "every member canvass" where everyone registered as a member will be visited. In the city, people tend to find that confrontational and they don't like it, but in some more rural areas, people love that approach. So, I backed away from thinking we should have the same plan for everyone and try instead to provide varied resources. I think of our approach as resource rich and rules thin.

Irene said that many traditional or routine fund-raising practices need to be handled differently "when fund raising for a religious entity."

We believe that what people give is their response to God for what they've been given in this world. Trying to increase understanding of that is a more delicate and difficult path to tread, but I believe deeply that that's the path we must tread. This is much more difficult than traditional fund raising because it requires a lot more education.

Another area that Irene noted required nontraditional thinking was in donor recognition. She said:

We have to be much more sensitive to the recognition we provide for big gifts. In God's eyes, your gift is judged by how much you have to give. I'm very uncomfortable when I know that someone gives what seems like a large amount but it is really only a drop in the bucket compared to their total assets and there are other people who have truly sacrificed to give, and, because their gift isn't as large, they don't get much recognition.

When asked about her future, Irene said that she would stay in that position, which she described as "a God-given opportunity for me in many ways," for as long as she thought she was helpful to the diocese.

Learning To Be Fund Raisers

In an open-ended question, we asked respondents to indicate how they had learned to be fund raisers. We used content analysis to sort all responses into nine categories and methods. Essentially, the data indicated that the majority of fund raisers—74 percent—had learned fund raising primarily in the same way that fund raisers have learned for the past thirty to forty years: on the job. Respondents' second most common method for learning, cited by 43 percent, was through professional development programs, which included any educational or training experiences not involving work on a formal degree (such as conferences, seminars, and university-based nondegree programs). Reading, mentoring, volunteering, networking, and participating in professional organization activities were methods for learning reported by 10 to 20 percent of respondents. Less than 10 percent of respondents cited formal education and consultants.

We compared the responses of men and women and found some slight differences. Not surprisingly, more women (21 per-

cent) than men (10 percent) cited volunteer experiences as a factor in their learning to be fund raisers. Men were slightly more
likely to cite on-the-job training, reading, and consultants as methods for learning. Women were slightly more likely to cite professional organization participation and networking as methods. We
also compared responses for methods of learning with age, years
of experience, and type of nonprofit organization and again found
only slight differences. The youngest respondents were more likely
to have learned through mentorships. Those in arts organizations
were the most likely to have learned about fund raising through
formal education. This may reflect the longer history of formal
programs in arts management, which have generally included
courses on fund raising or resource development.

We also asked respondents to indicate how they believed others can best learn to be fund raisers and sorted their responses into
the same nine categories or methods used for the question about
how they themselves had learned fund raising. In decreasing order,
the five most frequent responses were professional development
programs (58 percent), networking (46.1 percent), on-the-job
training (40 percent), reading (26.3 percent), and mentoring
(20.2 percent). The remaining four responses, cited by less than
10 percent, were formal education, volunteering, consultants, and
participating in professional organization activities. Men and
women viewed the best way for others to learn about fund raising
in slightly different ways. Women were more likely than men to
view networking, professional development programs, and reading as ways for others to learn, while men were more likely to cite
on-the-job training and experience. Age, years of experience, and
type of nonprofit organization did not seem to affect responses to
the question of how others should learn.

Comparing responses for how fund raisers learned and how
they think others should learn, it is clear that respondents did not
think the ways they themselves had learned were the best ways for
others to learn. Respondents recommended more professional development, reading, mentoring, and networking for others than
they themselves had had, less on-the-job training and volunteering, and fewer consultants. Of particular interest, despite the
growth in formal educational programs in nonprofit management
and fund raising and the success of these programs in placing

people, under 10 percent of respondents had learned fund raising through formal education, and only 7.3 percent of respondents indicated that this is the best way for others to learn. Formal educational programs in fund raising may be too new to have made a significant impact on the field, or respondents may believe there are too few programs to meet the need. It is also possible that respondents reject the notion that degree programs in fund raising are valuable and necessary. Finally, it is possible that those who did not learn fund raising through formal education do not see it as the way for others to learn.

In the past decade, a number of universities have established centers or programs for research and teaching in philanthropy, nonprofit organizations, and fund raising. The Nonprofit Academic Centers Council, an informal association of such centers, now lists twenty-four members. These centers emerged as the result of the growing awareness of the need and demand for specific education and training for careers in nonprofit organizations and voluntary associations. The growth of such academic programs reflects our belief that specific training in technical and ethical operations is essential if nonprofits are to improve performance, ensure survival, and retain the trust of those who support them. If fund-raising practice is to have a more professional orientation, technical and ethical standards must be enforced, and the body of knowledge that undergirds practice must be under continuous review and development. There must also be more formal mechanisms for transmitting knowledge, standards, and values of the field to those preparing for and serving in the field. If fund raising is to become more professional, practitioners must recognize the limitations imposed by heavy reliance on informal learning structures.

Improving Practice

To identify fund raisers' concerns about the field, we asked respondents to specify how they thought the practice of fund raising could be improved. A small number of respondents declined to respond, but no one wrote that there was no need for improvement. Overall, there were more than 2,600 responses to this item, indicating both that improving practice was a concern of practitioners and that they were not of one mind about what needed improving.

We sorted individual items into topics and listed them in decreasing order of frequency. The most frequently mentioned topics appeared more than fifty times each, representing 45 percent of the total responses to this survey item. The twelve topics and the number of times they appeared, in descending order, are:

- Promote ethics, integrity, and honesty in fund raising (194).
- Promote degree programs in fund raising (130).
- Provide education in fund raising for CEOs, board members, and volunteers (125).
- Make certification mandatory (115).
- Improve quality of and access to professional development and training programs (109).
- Promote continuing professional education (98).
- Provide formal programs for internships and mentoring (80).
- Promote better reporting and gift accounting (76).
- Increase commitment to present organization (69).
- Identify and sanction unethical fund raisers (60).
- Create more positive publicity for fund raisers (55).
- Standardize professional qualifications (51).

Because this list does not provide a sufficient overview of the topics, to further summarize responses, we used content analysis to sort topics into categories. The categories and frequencies are as follows:

- Education for fund raising (1,186 or 46 percent).
- Leadership from fund-raising managers (302 or 12 percent).
- Leadership from professional organizations (919 or 35 percent).
- Leadership from nonprofit organizations (199 or 8 percent).

A list of representative topics in each category follows:

Education for Fund Raising
  General (554)
- Promote overall continuing professional education.
- Promote degree programs in fund raising.
- Promote formal programs for internships and mentorships.
- Improve quality of and access to professional development and training programs.

- Improve quality of and increase professional development opportunities for senior and midcareer fund raisers.
- Increase training in fund raising in social work, public health, higher education, public administration, business, law, and communications degree programs.

Specific Skills (363)
- Fund-raising mechanics, basics, how-tos.
- Interpersonal and communication skills.
- Working with volunteers.
- Business skills.
- Cultivation, solicitation, and stewardship.
- Sales training.

Attitudes and Values (269)
- Increase commitment to present organization.
- Increase self-esteem and pride in fund raising.
- Accept that fund raising is not a profession.
- Eliminate complaining about negative perceptions of fund raising.

Leadership from Fund-raising Managers
General (57)
- Insist on ethics, integrity, and honesty in fund raising.
- Reduce administrative tasks.
- Reduce or eliminate telephone solicitations and direct mail solicitations.
- Involve other organizational members in fund raising.
- Reduce campaigns, campaign hype, and campaign mentality.
- Decrease reliance on volunteer solicitation.
- Eliminate staff solicitation.
- Reduce emphasis on credentials.
- Increase emphasis on mission and relationships.
- Eliminate sales mentality.
- Eliminate acceptance of unrealistic goals.
- Eliminate tendency to promise too much.

Human Resource Management (227)
- Compensation: Increase compensation, eliminate commissions, eliminate gender disparity, eliminate bonuses, provide more bonuses.
- Retention: Improve retention with better salaries and internal promotions.

- Recruitment and selection: Recruit more minorities, more young people, more people from the private sector; select staff based on proven track records.
- Performance: Improve communications about goals and expectations; evaluate performance based on dollars raised; evaluate performance based on activities, not dollars raised.

Fund-Raising Costs (18)
- Control fund-raising costs.
- Disclose fund-raising costs.

Leadership from Professional Organizations
General (95)
- Provide better comparative data for evaluation.
- Discourage use of term *fund raising*.
- Raise money to fund research in field.
- Improve marketing of membership in professional organizations.
- Increase cooperation among professional organizations.
- Eliminate old-boy network as leaders of professional organizations.

Certification (156)
- Make certification mandatory.
- Make certification more rigorous.
- Eliminate certification.
- Promote joint certification across professional organizations.

Standards and Values (222)
- Identify and sanction unethical fund raisers.
- Promote better reporting and gift accounting.
- Standardize professional qualifications.
- Increase the science of fund raising and reduce the art.
- Increase the art of fund raising and reduce the science.
- Standardize fund-raising titles and job descriptions.
- Promote peer reviews of fund raisers and programs.
- Set standards for commissions, bonuses, benefits, and perquisites.
- Set standards for fund-raising costs.

Promotion and Enhancement of the Fund-raising Field (446)
- Provide and promote education on fund raising for CEOs, board members, and volunteers.

- Create more positive publicity for fund raising.
- Increase public awareness of difference between ethical and unethical fund raising.

Leadership from Nonprofit Organizations (199)

- Provide adequate resources and support for fund raising.
- Promote internal appreciation of fund raisers.
- Conduct organizational assessment and set realistic goals for fund raising.
- Work to promote public confidence in the organization's mission.
- Involve fund raisers in organizational decision making.
- Increase organizational awareness that effectiveness takes time and involves more than the bottom line.
- Provide support for ethical fund raising.
- Promote formal coalitions among nonprofits to reduce competition and duplication of effort in fund raising.

The above list reflects concerns about multiple problems and considerable diversity of controversial and sometimes conflicting opinions. Also, the list suggests a fair level of discomfort among fund raisers about their colleagues and the field. The briefest summary of responses is that respondents thought the improvement of fund-raising practice can be achieved through more and better preparation and continued professional development of fund raisers and through more leadership in the field by fund-raising managers, professional organizations, and nonprofit organizations. Actually, all responses can be taken as a call for more leadership, since the education and continued professional development of most fund raisers is still the responsibility of professional organizations and more experienced practitioners in the field.

Ethical Concerns

The survey did not include specific questions regarding ethical concerns, but about 15 percent of the 2,600 responses to the question about how fund-raising practice can be improved related to ethics or had ethical connotations, such as "Make it a crime to steal from unsuspecting donors," and "Stop fund raisers from preying on old people." As indicated earlier, 194 respondents specifically noted that fund-raising practice could be improved if fund raising was more ethical or if fund raisers were more honest or had more integrity. Sixty respondents called for better internal regulation of the field to eliminate unethical fund raisers whom they described as charlatans, vultures, slime or sleaze balls, bad apples, crooks, snake oil salesmen, hustlers, and hucksters.

Almost every interviewee made some reference to ethical issues in fund raising and referred to ethical concerns both at the level of organizations and of individual fund raisers. Interviewees most often mentioned the ethical aspects of accountability issues, such as how gifts are counted and how fund-raising totals are reported; masking and failure to disclose fund-raising costs; misrepresentation of organizational capacity, resources, intentions, and priorities; and boards failing to oversee fund-raising activities or boards condoning inappropriate fund-raising practices.

Sometimes interviewees indicated they had experienced problems because they confronted organizational leaders about unethical practices and risked losing their influence and standing in their organizations. One interviewee stated:

> In a lot of organizations, fund raising can serve as the conscience, although that can be dangerous. In one job, I confronted the management staff about the misuse of gifts and didn't get invited to management meetings anymore.

Some interviewees were also concerned about the lack of appropriate and effective organizational responses to donors' efforts to unduly influence the organization or to donors' expectations of privileges in return for gifts. One interviewee was worried about "organizations collapsing into the substitution of 'quid pro quo interactions' for philanthropy." Another interviewee, noting that his present organization was "so bloody clean it's ridiculous," added:

> After my experiences involving fast-track, hard-nosed fund raising with some questionable legal activity, there was no way I was going to say no to the opportunity to work for a squeaky-clean organization. I've dealt with a lot of the sleazy stuff and I don't want to do that anymore. I wanted to get away from fund raising that crossed the line and looked for every loophole—sweetheart

deals, back-door deals, people making restricted gifts for illegal reasons—which goes on a lot.

Another interviewee reported:

We had an endowed chair held by a person whom the donor didn't like. The president told the dean to fire the one who held the chair or lose his own job. The person in the chair solved the problem by retiring. Now we are going through a search to fill the chair and the donor wants to be on the committee. The academic community knows the story so it has been hard to get good candidates. Where is it going to end?

Several interviewees noted that organizations with fund-raising programs that were more focused on the bottom line than on the mission were more likely to be negatively influenced by donors seeking to exercise inappropriate control.

Interviewees' concerns about the personal accountability of fund raisers referred mainly to fund raisers' roles in setting organizational practices and policies for gift accounting and reporting and in the ways in which fund raisers represent themselves on résumés, in job interviews, and in personal interactions with other fund raisers. One interviewee said, "Fund raisers are like many farmers. They're independent as hell and they always lie to you about how much they raised." Another interviewee reported that he sat on the search committee to fill the chief development officer's position at another organization. The committee eliminated four out of seven finalists after determining that those four candidates had significantly misrepresented their accomplishments to the committee. This interviewee was "appalled and embarrassed" by "how easy it was to detect the exaggerated claims" of the candidates, and he was even more "stunned by the fact that others on the search committee said that was what they expected to encounter in a search for a senior-level development position."

Interviewees had concerns about compensation practices, including salaries that were either too high or too low, commission-based compensation, how the promise of a bonus could affect decision making, and, especially, fund raisers who acquired material benefits as a result of their relationships with donors. One interviewee said:

An attorney will call and say, "There are three charities I can recommend to my client. What's in it for me if I direct this money to you?" If too much emphasis is placed on meeting goals, if I need that gift to make goal, or if I think my salary is too low, I might be tempted to do things that work against the good of the organization. For instance, I was the executor of a donor's will and received a fee of about $20,000. I turned that fee over to my organization. It was a very simple decision. Legally, I was entitled to the money; morally, I was not. If I didn't believe my salary was adequate, that $20,000 would have seemed very attractive.

Another interviewee said, "We have a lot of bright people in the field who haven't read the 501(c)(3) regulations or who haven't integrated them into their souls, so they find all kinds of ways to get around them." Several interviewees expressed concerns about taking "tainted money" and indicated that they personally had struggled to decide in some instances "if it is ethical for an organization to accept money acquired through less than honorable means to do good work with it and potentially exonerate the donor." Others raised questions about whether accepting such gifts would ultimately damage the reputation of the organization. One interviewee said she would accept any donation as long as there were no strings attached. She quoted singer Pat Boone, who was reported to have once said, "There's no tainted money—there 'jus tain't' enough of it."

Interviewees expressed numerous concerns about the ethical aspects of relationships with donors. One interviewee said:

I was involved in one situation that I call "Waltzing Matilda." The donor's name was Matilda and five of us development people from different organizations in the community were certainly waltzing her. I felt that was not ethical so I finally decided to stop going to see the lady because I didn't want to participate in that.

Some interviewees thought the most serious problem facing the fund-raising field was the expanded technological capacity to acquire personal information about donors. One interviewee said, "Fund raisers don't want to get caught in embarrassing situations or risk alienating donors but not enough fund raisers have a built-in repugnance about prying." Another interviewee said that indiscriminate solicitations by mail or telephone of people who have no interest in the organization are unethical, and others were concerned that sharing, selling, or stealing donor lists were common practices. Other interviewees mentioned problems associated with taking prospect information from one organization to another and advising donors to use "shaky tax loopholes."

Many fund raisers recognize that having organizational or professional standards and ethical codes is not sufficient to ensure ethical behavior if the standards and codes are accepted as minimum standards and if there are no means to enforce them. One interviewee said, "I believe that most people try very hard to do the right thing, but what is staggering is how much people don't know what the right thing is." Another noted, "If we were any good at policing our own, we wouldn't have bad apples, but we don't have a strong enough voice or the nerve to say 'this behavior will not be tolerated.'"

In general, interviewees seemed most personally distressed when they recounted situations in which another fund raiser deemed to have been guilty of unethical behavior continued to enjoy a position of prestige in the field. One person noted:

> A person in this city, well-educated, well-spoken, very knowledgeable, always on the speech circuit, always presenting at conferences, was hired here after an extensive search. He was in the position for six months. He made quite an impression on the rest of us because he seemed to work so hard, made so many calls, was so busy. Actually, he was operating his private consulting firm out of the office on our time. He was asked to leave when this was discovered and now works full time in his own business.

The interviewee explained that although the facts were widely known, this individual still held a prominent position in the local chapter of the professional organization. The interviewee stated, "Nothing will be done, and he's still the guru in this town."

More discussion of the ethical aspects of fund raising and respondents' concerns about these matters occurs in Chapter Eight, which identifies the most important and more difficult challenges facing the fund-raising field.

Chapter Seven

What Are the Best Fund Raisers Like?

This chapter presents information on the respondents' views of the personal characteristics, skills, and knowledge of the best fund raisers they knew.

Snapshots

These snapshots present two senior fund raisers—one with a dynamic personality and the other with outstanding management skills.

A Personality for Fund Raising

Theresa, fifty-nine years old at the time of the interview, was personable and energetic, with a good sense of humor and a hearty laugh. A Roman Catholic nun, she was the vice president for development at a Midwest Catholic college for women. She began her career as a teacher and became a principal at the age of twenty-eight. Following that, she became the personnel manager and, at the age of forty-three, the mother general of her order. She stepped down after eight years and returned to teaching at a college founded and operated by her order. When the president of the college asked her to assume the role of vice president for development, although she had never considered fund raising, she thought she might like the work because it involved meeting new people, it was challenging, and it would give her another opportunity to live out her commitment to her order and the college. She had been in that position for six years.

A product of Catholic schools, Theresa (like many of her class-mates) "found every occasion to get to know the boys" at a nearby military academy. She "played the field and had lots of boyfriends" and was engaged to be married when she finished high school. She also loved to sing and dance and had performed in many local pro-ductions. She remembered as a child arranging a dish towel over her hair, pretending it was the veil from a nun's habit, but she was not fully aware of her religious vocation until the summer after high school graduation. She had a conversation with a priest, a friend of the family, who reminded her that when she was in the third grade she said she was going to enter the convent. "When he left," she said, "I cried my heart out because I really had a deep conflict about it, but I had not allowed that conflict to come out. After that, I began to give it more thought and, by August, I told my mom and dad that I was going to the convent." It was a coura-geous decision to make—it meant moving more than a thousand miles away and giving up the life of wife and mother she had planned on. Although there were hard times, she had never re-gretted her decision.

There have been many changes in the Catholic Church during the time she had been a nun, and she noted that she was pleased about how different life was for nuns now compared to how it had been when she was younger:

> I really was happy when all of these changes started to come about because things seemed so oppressive before. We all dressed alike, we acted alike, and we could not allow our personalities to be different. That was a source of tension for me. I didn't like it, but there was no other way to make this life work but to follow the rules, which I did most of the time, but I, and some others, also pushed the limits. We did things that were not acceptable in those days. We marched in demonstrations. We moved first communion to fourth grade and confession to fifth grade, because it's far more important for a child to learn that God is loving than that God pun-ishes. We were persona non grata in some quarters—hippie nuns.

Theresa noted that her career experiences before fund raising required deep commitment, discipline, and risk taking, qualities that she believed now served her well as a fund raiser. She also thought that being a nun was useful to her as a fund raiser. She said:

I call myself the safe sex, because I am not competition for either men or women but I know how to get into men's offices. The line I use is "I'd like your advice." Men love nothing better than to give advice. That gets my foot in the door but they know I really want something more. They know I raise money. I'm in every community activity that I can be in. I was the first woman in the Rotary when they allowed women in about three years ago. I don't mind going alone to dinners or to meetings, but if they say to bring a guest, that's not a problem. If a sister goes with me, she knows there is a basic ground rule. She knows not to hang around me because I'll be working the crowd. I'll introduce her but then she's on her own.

Relating a preference that is common among many fund raisers (Duronio and Loessin, 1991), Theresa said:

The hard part of this job is that supervision of staff keeps me from getting out on the street, and my favorite place is out on the street. I love to be where people are. I like to get a minimum of five appointments a week outside the office. I wish I didn't have to do any supervision so I could be out there raising money. I find supervision more tolerable when I have good staff working for me. I like to hire people who are outgoing, raring to go, ready to give all they have. I also need good staff because fund raising is still new to me, after six years. It seems like I'm building the bicycle and riding it at the same time. I learn on the job. I use my staff and we brainstorm ideas.

Theresa emphasized that the ability to be persuasive was probably most important in fund raising. She said:

A few years ago, the owner of a liquor company in town offered me a sales job with his company, which I thought was funny. He said he thought I could do a great job selling liquor. I had never thought of sales as a career, but he's right—I could, if I wanted to. I could also raise money for the hospital. In fact, they offered me a job a couple of years ago, but I said no because I'm strongly connected to this college. I could sell anything or raise money for any cause. Just don't ask me to stay behind a desk. You might as well put me in a box or lock me up. I could not handle that.

Saying, "I've always wanted to be a priest," Theresa said she objected to "those women who think they are highly liberated who want to get into the church and be like the priests of today." She added:

> I don't want to perpetuate that model because it's too hierarchical. If women merely take on that role, how have we improved things? We would just be following the white male model. The reason women should be in the priesthood is not because we can do what men can do but because we can bring something different to the priesthood. It's true in fund raising, too, as women come into the field and achieve higher-status positions. We will shortchange the field if we simply model ourselves after the men who previously held all these higher positions. I think women are more likely to share responsibility and credit and to use people wherever their talents lie. These are good objectives for the priesthood and fund raising.

She planned to stay in her present job for at least five more years. The college was about to start an $11 million campaign. She thought she would complete the campaign and then "say farewell" to the formal position but not to the role of being an advocate for the college and her order.

Serious About Management

At the time of the interview, Andrew was in his early forties and had been in development positions for ten years at a prestigious southern liberal arts college. Andrew reluctantly left a nine-year career in public school teaching, which he loved, because he wanted to earn more money to support his growing family. He believed that teaching was an excellent preparation for advancement work, observing that "Development officers who don't have a sense of themselves as educators need to find something else to do."

During the planning for a capital campaign, Andrew was asked to add the annual fund to his alumni responsibilities. He eventually was promoted to director of development with oversight for all development activities, and then to director of campaigns—which included both ongoing development activities and special campaign responsibilities. In strong contrast to Theresa, introduced in the previous snapshot, Andrew was very interested in the management of a complex fund-raising operation. He related that the development operation, with plans under way for a major campaign, grew "from a small operation in which it was easy not to step on one another's toes to a much larger, sophisticated operation with a huge assignment."

This growth caused a significant problem in "pushing the work down." He said:

> When we were smaller, this was a top-down organization where the vice president was the primary outside person and everyone else supported that effort. With the charge to raise $150 million in five years, we knew we had to have many people out making calls, but we weren't very good at pushing those assignments down. None of us really knew how to spread the responsibility for raising money across a very talented but fairly young staff of about thirty people.

Pressure to push the work down also came from the younger staff, who complained that they were getting neither enough responsibility to make their jobs interesting nor the experience they needed to advance professionally. This, Andrew noted, was "a very healthy attitude" that he wanted to encourage.

He hired a management development consultant who met with the entire staff and initiated programs to improve teamwork and communication. Over a period of twenty-four months, the consultant also led the staff in a project to redesign all jobs "so that the load was shared and the chances for advancement were real and well defined." The process also included group participation in planning at several levels: for overall fund-raising programs, for the campaign, and for individual performance appraisals. The performance appraisal process involved annual goal setting and quarterly evaluations for each staff member. Andrew pointed out that theirs was the only office in the college to use such an appraisal system and to give merit-based salary increases. He continued:

> We reward people who work hard and sometimes we have to tell folks that they are not getting raises at all. Facing the reality of merit-based pay increases has been stimulating for some staff and unpleasant for others.

Andrew initiated varied professional development activities for staff. One such activity involved brown-bag lunchtime sessions during which faculty members talk about their work to advancement staff. At these sessions, academics and the college, not fundraising techniques or strategies, were the focus. Andrew also held an annual advancement retreat that included outside speakers. Last year, Andrew noted:

> We invited two women from the national philanthropic and higher education communities to lead sessions on the national context of our college's campaign. Our fund raisers need to understand what national leaders in higher education and philanthropy are thinking. Our folks know how to go out and ask for money. What we need to constantly improve is our ability to translate the wonderful things going on in our classrooms to our donors. We also deliberately chose women this year because most of the younger staff we hire are women and most of the senior staff are men, and that's a problem sometimes. It's important for our young women to have someone to listen to other than gray-haired men, and it's also good for us men to learn from successful women.

Andrew appeared most energized when talking about developing staff and the connection of staff development with increased fund-raising success—a system based on careful planning and monitoring, close communication with supervisors, and merit-based increases. He said:

> When talking to somebody on staff about a salary increase, ultimately I'm saying, "This is how much we value you." Rigor, discipline, and honesty about the market drive our conversations here about remuneration. I encourage our people to be on the lookout for other opportunities. I like it when our staff get other offers and we can negotiate to keep them. We lost a young woman last week who is going to be director of development somewhere else. When she left, she said, "I'm going to get some great experience, and I'll be back." She was saying to me, "I may get your job!" Now that's the attitude I really like!

Andrew acknowledged that staff continuity was important in fund raising but said he most wanted "a lively, yeasty, boiling, ambitious organization." Although he expected fund-raising staff to have a personal commitment to education and to care about the college, he did not expect staff to stay out of loyalty. He said:

Nine times out of ten, the people who stay out of loyalty are not the people I want. I want productive, ambitious individuals and if they'll give me four to six good years, I'm happy.

In Andrew's opinion, retention of fund-raising staff depends more on organizational practices than on individual fund raisers. He noted:

I spend a lot of time telling our vice president for finance that we better recognize the impact of the external market or we will lose our people. It is irrelevant to our staff what somebody in some other college department earns. What is relevant is what the hospital in town pays fund raisers. This institution needs to pay its people what they are worth in the market. In return, if the institution needs to be tough with us and impose zero-based budgeting and challenging goals, that's fine, but they've got to pay us competitively or we'll leave.

Regarding the future, Andrew said:

I have become more interested in fund raising as a profession than I ever thought I would be. Earlier, I thought that my primary allegiance would be to this college, and that I would be more interested in accepting another administrative position here than I would be in moving on. I have had other opportunities to consider here. But, interestingly, as I get better at what I do, I am not willing to walk away from this expertise. My guess is that in five years I will be even less likely to give up this career. Five years from now I might well be in a fund-raising role at another institution. That is a real evolution in terms of how I look at my work.

Characteristics of Effective Fund Raisers

There is a keen interest among many fund raisers in identifying what good fund raisers are like, what they know, and what they can do. As indicated earlier, some of those involved in the original plans for this project hoped this research would provide a psychometric profile of good fund raisers. A profile that specified the qualities of effective fund raisers would assist in selection and promotion of fund-raising staff, help define the special expertise and contributions of the field, and promote a more positive image of fund raisers.

To identify the characteristics of good fund raisers, it would first be necessary to identify good fund raisers—a challenge that exceeded the resources and scope of this project. Although both the AHP and the NSFRE have programs to confer certification upon fund raisers who meet a set of comprehensive requirements, it is estimated that less than one-quarter of members of these professional organizations hold certifications. Additionally, evidence from this research and elsewhere indicates that there is no consensus among fund raisers that certification is a necessary and sufficient criterion for identifying the most effective people working in the field.

One of the most problematic aspects in specifying the criteria of effective performance in fund raising is the dramatic diversity of the environments in which fund raisers work. Large, affluent nonprofit organizations acquire more money in private support and have more resources—including funds for higher salaries for fund raisers—to expend in the process of raising money. Therefore, what first appear to be rather straightforward measures of a fund raiser's success—total money raised and salary earned—must be interpreted in the context of the nonprofit organizations in which they were achieved. Other characteristics of nonprofit organizations and their fund-raising programs also affect the interpretation of measures such as salary earned or total dollars raised. The history of the fund-raising program is one such characteristic. Most experienced fund raisers agree that an organization in a start-up phase, an organization just completing its first major campaign, or an organization with a fully mature comprehensive fund-raising program require different fund-raising approaches. Clearly, some individuals could be outstanding in one of those situations and failures in another. Perhaps some individuals could be successful in any of those situations, and some individuals could not be successful in any of them.

Relative to the task of specifying what measures actually define effective performance in fund raising, in addition to the way in which nonprofit environments can vary and the impact this variation can have on the work of fund raising, there is the additional complexity of the variety of roles fund raisers perform in their organizations (Kelly, 1991, 1994). After a thorough review of the fund-raising literature, Worth and Asp (1994) determined that authors in the field generally conceptualize fund raisers as *salesperson* (the fund raiser's primary function is direct solicitation); *catalyst* (the fund raiser brings about the direct solicitation but stays in the background); *manager* (the fund raiser focuses primarily on management, organization, and direction of internal resources); and *leader* (the fund raiser may function in any or all of the first three roles but also serves as a key participant in organizational decision making). Although all those who identify themselves as fund raisers are engaged in some way in raising money from private sources, how they function in those roles and what they actually do varies a great deal. As fund raisers' roles vary, so will the qualifications and skills necessary to perform those roles.

Because of all these complexities, developing valid and reliable operational measures to identify effective fund raisers was beyond the scope of this project. Nevertheless, although it was not possible to demonstrate an empirical relationship between characteristics of fund raisers and successful performance, it was possible to collect information about the characteristics, skills, and knowledge believed to underlie successful performance that would not only be useful in its own right and but might also form a basis for further research.

What Fund Raisers See as Their Best

On the survey, we asked the participants: "Think of the fund-raising professional that you believe is the most competent and successful of all those you know. In the designated sections below, please list up to three (A) personal characteristics or traits, (B) learned skills, and (C) areas of professional knowledge that you believe have contributed most to this person's effectiveness." A footnote defined professional knowledge as "facts and concepts that practitioners in a certain field know, often learned in formal training, that are generally not considered to be common knowledge among those not in the field."

We wanted to know what fund raisers themselves thought were the primary characteristics of the most competent and successful people in their field. Instead of asking them to describe an ideal fund raiser, that is, to think of what fund raisers should be like, we framed the question to call on respondents' actual experience and first-hand knowledge. Asking the question in this way, by specifying "the most competent and successful fund raisers" respondents knew, we hoped to capture what fund raisers admired in each other—especially the qualities they associated with successful fund raising. We also attempted to guide respondents to differentiate personal, skill, and knowledge characteristics, to determine if respondents believed that personal characteristics, skills, and professional knowledge all contributed to successful fund raising. We used content analysis techniques to organize, summarize, and analyze the individual responses—more than eleven thousand in all—this survey item generated. We developed seven categories for responses for personal characteristics, five categories for skills, and four categories for professional knowledge.

Personal Characteristics

The seven categories for responses for personal characteristics include:

- *Personality characteristics.* Traits describing demeanor and manner, including items such as personable, sincere, and cheerful.
- *Workstyle characteristics.* Traits describing approaches to work, including items such as hard-working, prompt, and team-oriented.
- *Ethical characteristics.* Traits describing character as differentiated from personality, including items such as integrity, is ethical, and honorable.
- *Commitment characteristics.* Traits describing commitment, including items such as committed to organization (fund-raising field, mission), desire to help people, and zealous.
- *Cognitive characteristics.* Traits describing mental characteristics, including items such as intelligent, intuitive, and scholarly.
- *Self-Concept characteristics.* Traits reflecting respondents' ideas of the self-perceptions of the fund raisers they described, including items such as self-confident, has self-esteem, and self-demanding.
- *Background characteristics.* Traits regarding personal background, including items such as wealthy, graduate of the school, and lifelong member of the community.

Skills

The five categories for all responses for skills included:

- *Communication skills.* Items such as overall communication, public speaking, and listening.
- *Management skills.* Items such as organizational skills, planning, and time management—which may refer to the handling of one's own job, the oversight of programs, other staff, and volunteers, or both.
- *Fund-raising skills.* Items such as solicitation, working with board members, and getting appointments.
- *Cognitive skills.* Items such as memorizing, analyzing, and clear thinker.
- *Other skills.* Items falling into a catch-all category; for example, can sleep on airplanes, good golfer, and works within system.

Professional Knowledge

The three categories for all responses for professional knowledge include:

- *Fund-raising knowledge.* Items such as all aspects of fund raising, tax and legal knowledge, and gift administration.
- *Management knowledge.* Items such as finance, computer technology, and organizational behavior.
- *Background knowledge.* Items falling into a catch-all category; for example, human behavior, a specific educational background (such as law degree, business degree, degree in the arts), and private sector experience.

Survey Results

Table 7.1 displays the frequency of response for categories for personal characteristics, skills, and professional knowledge.

The table shows only the total number of times respondents reported an item in the category because there were few differences overall in responses from men and women or in responses from fund raisers in different nonprofit subsectors. This indicates

Table 7.1. All Categories of Responses.

Type	Category	Number	Percent
PK	Fund-raising knowledge	2,080	17.6
SK	Communication skills	1,837	15.5
SK	Management skills	1,606	13.6
PC	Personality characteristics	1,466	12.4
SK	Fund-raising skills	1,368	11.6
PC	Workstyle characteristics	1,231	10.4
PC	Ethical characteristics	734	6.2
PC	Commitment characteristics	450	3.8
PK	Management knowledge	281	2.4
PK	Background knowledge	241	2.0
PC	Cognition characteristics	215	1.8
PC	Self-concept characteristics	173	1.5
SK	Cognition skills	92	0.8
PC	Background characteristics	24	0.2
SK	Other skills	23	0.2
	Total	11,821	100.0

Note: PC = personal characteristics; SK = skills; PK = professional knowledge

that conceptual understanding of the qualities believed to underlie effective fund-raising performance do not vary between men and women or across nonprofit subsectors. For the fifteen categories we developed, 81 percent of all responses fell into the top six categories, indicating that respondents most often described effective fund raisers in terms of their fund-raising knowledge, their communication, management, and fund-raising skills, and their personality and workstyle characteristics.

All individual items reported one hundred or more times are listed in order of frequency in Table 7.2. This list of thirty-four items, similar to those reported by others (see, for example, Panas, 1988), representing about 56 percent of all responses, is a summary of what respondents most frequently believed the best fund raisers knew, could do, and were like.

Table 7.2. Most Frequently Reported Specific Responses.

Type	Response	Number
PK	Planned giving	396
SK	Organizational skills	393
SK	Communication skills	350
SK	Writing	333
SK	Making the ask	311
SK	Listening	301
PC	Commitment to cause or organization	297
PC	Has integrity	288
PK	All areas of fund raising	259
PC	Honest	241
SK	Interpersonal skills	233
PK	Tax or legal knowledge related to giving	229
PK	Knowledge of cause or organization	200
SK	Management	197
SK	Working with volunteers	194
PK	Campaign knowledge	180
SK	Solicitation	171
SK	Motivating others	165
PC	Ethical	144
PK	Marketing	133
PC	Intelligent	127
SK	Grantsmanship	124
SK	Verbal skills	122
PC	Self-confident	119
PC	Personable	116
SK	Planning	114
PC	Enthusiastic	113
PK	Annual funds	113
SK	Presentation skills	108
PC	Outgoing	108
PC	Sincere	105
PK	Major gifts	104
PK	Finance	103
PC	Friendly	103

Note: PC = personal characteristics; SK = skills; PK = professional knowledge

As described by their peers, the best fund raisers were ethical, smart, committed people who were also friendly and sincere. They were knowledgeable about fund raising and also about their organizations. They were skilled in all forms of communication, interpersonal relationships, and fund-raising activities.

Only seven responses to this survey question did not have entirely positive connotations. They included: chameleon, cocky, egotistical, glib, ingratiating, arrogant, and opportunistic (two times). One respondent especially wanted to express her ambivalence about this survey item. Instead of filling in the blanks, she wrote:

> I have a problem with this item. There is an issue you are not addressing: At what cost is this person a "best" fund raiser? The "best" fund raiser I know is my boss. He is an excellent fund raiser and I greatly admire his abilities. However, he is the "best" at the expense of his staff. He is manipulative, sets unrealistic goals, expects his staff to accomplish everything, and to have it done almost immediately, yet he does not involve us in planning. He is not a team player nor a team leader. To him, the "almighty dollar" takes precedence over office management, organizational skills, and planning. He creates chaos and a very stressful working environment. We all are committed to the institution and our jobs and take extreme care in what we do, yet receive no appreciation or acknowledgment from him. Our highest performance is simply taken for granted. I think it is very important for a fund raiser to be balanced—to understand that the process is just as important as the bottom line. Without the proper balance, the staff will burn out and leave and the institution's image will suffer. Sooner or later, this will affect relationships with donors and the amount of money raised.

This respondent made the important point that in the genuine best fund raiser, positive personal characteristics, fund-raising and management skills, and broad professional knowledge will be integrated to promote the long-term advantage of the organization. This respondent also made the important point that the bottom line is not the only aspect of fund raising that can affect the well-being of the organization. While we agree strongly with these points, we also think it is important to note that the respondent selected as the best fund raiser she knew someone who was not actually successful in all areas.

Summary of Best Fund Raisers

Overall, what have we learned about how respondents conceptualized "the right stuff" of fund raising, and what is the value of this information? In general, the data indicate that respondents had high expectations of their fund-raising colleagues, prized traits that indicate strong characters and warm personalities, and acknowledged the importance of skills and knowledge in successful fund raising. Respondents also conveyed a strongly value-driven orientation to the field and insight about the sensitive interplay of the art and science of fund raising. Perhaps the information is as valuable for what it reveals about the respondents as for how it defines effective fund raisers.

There are several limitations to the value of this information. One reflects the major limitation of the entire study—only fund raisers who are members of professional organizations were surveyed. Another is that these characteristics are quite broad and, except for the skills and knowledge specific to fund raising, describe what most employers would agree represents an ideal for employees in any role. A third limitation, already noted, is that the information provided by respondents, although they were asked to think of "the most competent and successful" fund raiser they knew, does not actually demonstrate any empirical relationship between any of the noted characteristics and successful fund raising. However, an additional value of this information is that it provides a starting point for additional research to define and measure the relationship between these characteristics and effective fund raising.

| # Key Issues in Fund Raising

Drawing from all the data from the research, we have identified what we believe are the critical issues facing the fund-raising field, issues that were first listed in Chapter One. In this chapter, we discuss each of these issues in some detail.

Snapshots

The five fund raisers described here are all quite unlike one another, but what they have in common is a strong and proud sense of themselves as effective fund raisers. There is also something about each of them or their careers that might, in the minds of some fund raisers, prevent the people in this group from being identified as models for the field.

Strong Feelings About Commitment

Lucy was twenty-six at the time of the interview and had worked in fund raising for three years. She worked for a symphony in a large city, as the assistant to the director of development with a special assignment in planned gifts. After leaving college, Lucy accepted a job at a bank in a large city where she marketed tax-deferred products. As a season ticket holder who loved the symphony, she was pleased to meet a member of the symphony's board of directors through her job. One day the board member mentioned that the symphony had an opening in the planned giving area. Lucy got the job and divided her time among administrative responsibilities, preparation of materials, event planning, and providing support to volunteers. She earned under $25,000.

Lucy had especially strong opinions about the value of organizational commitment in fund raising. She said:

I have a problem at fund raisers' professional meetings because most people come to network for better jobs. I see a lot of job-hopping going on, and that bothers me. I find it hard to believe that people who change jobs every two years have real heartfelt commitment to their organizations. I would not apply for an opening at the theater or the museum just because it would mean a promotion for me. Personally, I couldn't care less about the theater or the museum, and I couldn't ask people for money for them. If I ever leave the symphony, I will probably leave fund raising.

Lucy was concerned about the credibility of fund raisers who frequently changed jobs. She said:

It's those kinds of people who give fund raising a bad name. I hate watching fund raisers play musical chairs. I don't see how you can put your heart and soul into an institution when you are using it as a stepping stone to get some place else, and fund raising, if your heart and soul aren't in it, is not respectable. It's manipulative and dishonorable.

Lucy also thought that people should become fund raisers out of a desire to work for a specific cause. She said:

I don't think that we should encourage people to want to be fund raisers just because there are openings in the field or because it is a good career. I can't imagine that people would take a fund-raising course and then say, "Now I need a cause." What are they going to do, just answer any old ad and then tell people that they think the National Hubcap Society is the greatest thing in the world? I hope people who do that are only a very small percentage of the field.

Lucy only wanted people who loved the symphony to contribute. She said:

I don't want to take money from somebody walking down the street. I want to take money from somebody who believes in the symphony as much as I do. I don't even like to see board members ask for donations from friends who don't care about the symphony at all. It's not the same.

She was also critical of people of means who regularly attended the symphony's programs but who were not generous donors.

There was no question about Lucy's commitment to the symphony, but some fund raisers would raise questions both about her commitment to the fund-raising field and about her effectiveness. Although she bridled when a corporate prospect suggested that the symphony's fund-raising staff was only interested in sustaining the symphony so that "rich people can continue to enjoy themselves at concerts," she was not particularly effective at articulating the case for support for the symphony, particularly at a time when so many others thought that raising money for the arts was difficult. Her "love it or leave it" attitude might help her to be effective with others who felt the way she did, but it would not help her if she was ever called upon to win nonbelievers over to the cause.

Potential in Need of Guidance

Mark was thirty-four at the time of the interview and had been in fund raising for about eight years. He had just begun his fifth job in fund raising and earned about $43,000. When he was still a college student, he volunteered to make calls for the university's phonothon. He did such a good job that he was offered a part-time position in the phonothon program and the part-time job soon became a full-time position. Mark's original career objective was to be in sales, maybe to sell computers and then become a district manager. After starting in fund raising, which he thought of as a "kind of sales," he realized that he liked nonprofit fund raising because it meant helping people. He began to think that helping people would be more satisfying than selling a product.

While in Job #1, he joined a professional organization and, after about a year of networking at chapter meetings, he got Job #2 in a new development program at a nearby hospital. After working in Job #2 for about a year, he said:

> I started seeing some things that I didn't care for, things that made me uncomfortable about how the organization spent charitable dollars. For instance, expense accounts there were extravagant. That raised a question about whether I wanted to continue working for someone I didn't always agree with.

Again, by networking through the professional organization, Mark met the fund raiser who is now his boss, who recruited him to Job #3 in another state. At this job for a hospital system, he provided fund-raising consulting to the system's individual hospitals. He came to dislike the job because he worked with the hospitals' development directors rather than directly with volunteers or donors. After three years, he moved to Job #4 as the director of development for a small hospital where "relationships started to wane and things just didn't work out." He also began to think that "going from a large multifacility organization down to a single small hospital wasn't necessarily best for my career."

His boss from Job #3 had since relocated to still another state to take a vice presidency; he recruited Mark to join him as director of development in Job #5. At this job a few months, Mark thought that his boss would leave within three years and he might then be promoted to the position of vice president. He was primarily interested in higher salary, but he was also interested in greater responsibilities. He said:

> I think I have more talents than fund raising to offer the institution. By moving up to the vice president's level, I'd be part of the team that makes bigger decisions. When the time comes, I think I can be an asset to an organization at that level.

After reaching the level of vice president, Mark thought he would stay in that position for five to seven years and then leave to start his own business. Although he was certain that he would operate his own business someday, he did not know what kind of business it would be, but he did not think he would want to have a fund-raising consulting business. His motivation for starting a business was to be able to leave it to his children. He also thought that he would work as a volunteer after starting his own business as a way to offer his fund-raising expertise to others.

Mark was charming, enthusiastic, and probably a genuinely caring, hardworking person. Although he clearly was motivated by material and status rewards, he expected to work hard and wanted to help others. He held a responsible position in his professional organization and had always contributed time and effort to the professional organization. In spite of his good qualities, Mark will appear to many to lack the appropriate values for a career in fund raising. However, instead of concluding that this is Mark's individual failure, an alternative interpretation could be that fund raising's methods of socializing newcomers has failed him. Mark has not had the benefit of appropriate socialization in the values of the field—in this case, placing commitment to the organization above career advancement. Mark's experiences with those who have served as mentors and in participating in professional organization activities do not seem to have provided sufficient clarification of the values of those with the highest standards and expectations for the field.

Big Bird's Mother

Maggie, at forty-seven, was vice president for development for the public television station in a southern city. After sixteen years in development, all of it in public radio and television, she earned about $72,000. Before entering the development field, she was a self-taught systems analyst and computer programmer. She worked in banking as one of the pioneers in the development and marketing of electronic funds transfer systems, which ultimately took her into a management position in bank telemarketing. After her husband's business took them to another state, Maggie used her marketing skills to get the job as chief development officer at the television station.

When asked why she stayed in fund raising, Maggie acknowledged that the rewards came both from the satisfaction of increasing financial support for the station and from the personal recognition she received. She said:

> This is one of the most gratifying jobs in development. I think I play a role in helping people to live better lives by providing education and entertainment and I get the greatest kind of payback. I get on the air and ask for money and instantly the phones start ringing. That's instant gratification—instant proof of how well I am performing my job.

Maggie observed that most fund raisers have behind-the-scenes roles in their jobs but she enjoyed being in front of the camera.

"My husband says that when I see a red traffic light, I think that means I'm on camera and should start talking," she joked. Maggie said that because people see her on the air, they feel as if they already know her, which she saw as very helpful in beginning to establish personal relationships with donors. She said:

> We have the advantage in television. On the air, we go instantly into people's homes. I get fan mail all the time. People call me to pledge and add that they loved the dress I was wearing or that green is really my color. Once, I appeared on the air with Big Bird for a pledge drive for kids' programs. I went to the grocery store later that day, and I heard a little girl behind me say, "Mom, that's Big Bird's mother. I saw her and Big Bird on TV." Her mother told me how much she appreciated what our station did for her daughter, and I had the opportunity to emphasize how much her support could mean to the station.

Maggie had no plans to leave the station. She said:

> I am part of the top management team that is influencing the direction of this station. I have gotten job offers in other development areas, but as long as I can grow and as long as I can contribute, I'd like to be a part of this team. I could raise money for medical research or to help provide services to the elderly, because those are things I feel strongly about, but I'd miss the limelight.

Maggie's enjoyment of the limelight may concern those who feel strongly that the best fund raisers avoid seeking personal recognition for their work. On the other hand, Maggie's story is an excellent example of a perfect fit between organization and fund raiser.

Commitment to the Field

Louis was sixty years old and had been in fund raising for about twenty-five years. He had worked for three higher education institutions, a medical foundation, and an organization for the blind before joining his present organization, a seminary in a northeastern city. He had been in this job for two years and earned about $48,000.

After finishing college, he taught high school for eight years in the Midwest before he "sort of happened into fund raising." He explained:

> I had the opportunity to go back to my alma mater as director of alumni relations. I was interested because I thought I was starting to sound more like a tape recorder than a teacher. When I took the position, fund raising was the least attractive part of the job, and I decided just to endure that part. As time went on, we got into a capital campaign and fund raising soon became what I liked most. I saw fund raising in a different way as I could see the real impact that charitable giving had and the very visible and tangible results of that campaign.

After more than six years, because he had a boss who had no plans to leave, Louis decided that it was time for him to move on. He ended up in Alaska where he had "four great years" before needing to return to the Midwest for family reasons. He took a two-year position as campaign director for a private college and, when that job ended, he moved to a job at a medical foundation where he stayed for seven years. He left for a promotion as director of development for a hospital foundation, where he had a serious conflict with a board member. After two years, he left there and went to an organization for the blind. When he had been there two years, the organization merged with another organization and his job was eliminated. He moved from the organization for the blind into his present job.

Louis had provided years of service to his professional organization. He said:

> I'm concerned that too many senior people have the attitude that professional organizations are only for people new in the field or for those looking for a new job. I think those of us who have grown in the field have a responsibility to give back.

He currently chaired the ethics committee for his local chapter, which he had done in another city as well. He was interested in the area of fund-raising ethics not only because he thought it had grown in importance as the field had expanded but also because he was committed to the fund-raising field. He thought that a strong core of ethical practice was critical to the continued growth of the field and the long-term best interests of nonprofit organizations dependent upon voluntary support.

Louis believed that the most serious and frequent ethical problems facing fund raisers involved conflicts between an individual's self-interest and the interest of the organization, such as when a fund raiser had the opportunity to acquire personal benefits as a result of a relationship with a donor. He added:

> All of us in this business have had opportunities to personally benefit from friendships with donors. I know one individual at a college who was aware that he was named in a donor's will. He ended up with a handsome amount. I think that's wrong. I once was offered a grand piano by a lady in California. I would have loved to take it, but it would not have been right because I did not have a relationship with her for personal benefit. I was there for the institution. It would be wrong to use that relationship for my benefit.

Other ethical problems occur because some fund raisers "act with questionable ethics in order to land the big gift because it is going to look good on their résumé."

Louis thought that "multiyear, broad-based contracts between fund-raising employees and their institutions" was one way in which ethical problems in fund raising could be reduced. He added:

> I favor contracts that spell out what is expected of the development person and also what he or she in turn can expect from the leadership of the institution. I think contracts would give fund raisers an element of security that would keep them from constantly looking where to go next or resorting to unethical practices to improve their results. I don't know of anybody who has had such a contract but something concrete on paper that reminds trustees, presidents, and development officers of those agreements and obligations would be helpful.

After reviewing a preliminary working paper on this research, Louis wrote back to say:

> After reading your report, I was struck by the frequency with which fund raisers are negatively judgmental of our peers. I find

disconcerting the criticism of others' salaries, certification, how
hard others don't work, and the lack of dedication. I wonder
whether the basis for such judgments are valid. Maybe it's a case
of unconscious jealousies of the people with high salaries and visi-
bility in the spotlight. It hurts me to see us criticizing each other.
Perhaps this is yet another obstacle to overcome in the search for
true professionalism.

Some fund raisers may be critical of Louis's career, taking the
position that he had changed jobs too often, or that, after twenty-
five years in the field, he had not reached the highest levels of responsibility, influence, and rewards. Louis' career included longer
and shorter jobs, but also was marked by a number of job hazards
that others will confirm are fairly common in fund raising, such as
jobs being eliminated because organizations have merged or campaigns have ended, and conflicts with board members or key executives. In spite of the fact that Louis had not reached the highest
levels in fund raising, he was nevertheless one of the most quietly
compelling of all interviewees. By virtue of his tenure in the field,
his commitment and regard for the field, his statesmanlike approach to issues facing the field, and his generous nature, he had
the resources to be able to give a lot back—and he did.

Competitive and Committed to Integrity

At forty-seven, Randall was executive vice president of a fund-raising
consulting firm in a Western city. He earned over $100,000 per year.
After graduating from college, Randall taught junior high school
for a short time before going to work for a national nonprofit
human services agency. He stayed with this agency for thirteen years
and held a number of progressively responsible positions. He explained, "My strong suit was taking over regional offices that were
in serious financial and programmatic trouble and doing turn-
arounds." He did not have a positive opinion of his former employer. He said:

> When I would leave the room at a major conference, I could not
> wait to get my name tag off because I didn't want to be associated
> with my peers because of the level of incompetence. There were

too many people in that organization who had no desire to change, to learn anything new, or take any risks. That was very frustrating. I knew I was in the wrong business.

Although he earned a high salary (about which he said, "I'm glad the local United Way never found out what I made"), he decided to leave.

He took a sales job and, in a few months, he realized that he did not want to work in a for-profit environment where "whether you make widgets or not doesn't mean anything." He accepted a position with a fund-raising consulting firm, where his first assignment was managing a campaign for a museum. He said:

I was a resident director living on-site in a remote community. You may quote me directly: I would sooner pump gas than be a resident manager ever again. Living in an apartment away from my wife and children was not my thing, but I was so successful at that project that I immediately moved into the number two slot in the company. Then I sold business and managed projects. I enjoyed that very much, and do to this day.

He left that firm after three years, because:

That company's philosophy was to make as great a profit with as little effort as possible. The guy who owned the company was driven by greed and dishonesty, and I have to get up and look at myself every day in the mirror. If I conduct a feasibility study and see that there is not a realistic campaign there or the leadership is not in place, then I want to recommend the steps necessary to bring about change for campaign success down the road. Of course, that doesn't put an immediate dollar in your pocket. This company philosophy was to grab as much business as you can whether it's right or not. I refused to keep doing that.

Eventually, he joined his present company, where he had been for over nine years. He described his boss as "the most honest person I have ever worked for." He had advanced to the position of vice president and did not foresee leaving this firm.

About problems in the fund-raising field, Randall said:

There are too many people who hang degrees and certifications on their walls and declare themselves the leaders of the field. Then they draw a line to declare who is good and who isn't. That is like the inmates running the asylum. Too often, those in leadership positions in the professional societies become the in-group but it is not necessarily those that we ought to emulate. Their lives are driven by their success in this hierarchical structure rather than by their success back where their check is being cut. Certainly, bona fide credentials are important, but they are enhancements to the more important qualities of good fund raisers—honesty, integrity, and the ability to communicate.

Randall was especially critical of turnover in fund raising. He said:

There's a tremendous amount of rollover going on. I've been as motivated by career advancement as the next person but it's wrong if your focus is to do the best job you can so you're invited some place else. Track records in fund raising are a nightmare to sort out because the reality and perception are often a million miles apart. There are a lot of people in the field inflating their own track records. Unless good development professionals and good counseling firms take an aggressive stand and refuse to hire people who do that, they're going to drag all of us down. In development, you cannot breeze into town, spend two years, breeze on to your next job, and claim to have done any service for your employer. You can't do this very personal thing called fund raising on a ticket through town.

Randall indicated that turnover not only hurt fund raisers but also hurt the whole process of philanthropy. He said, "Development fails in this country far more than it needs to simply because fund raisers aren't around long enough to ask, and that failure is an indictment of the development profession."

Randall conveyed some of his attitudes about raising money. He said:

I don't just want donors' money. More than their money, I want their time and talent. I think it was Haldeman who had the famous brass plaque on his desk that said: "When you have them by the balls, their hearts and minds will follow." In philanthropy, when you have their time and talent, the financial resources will follow.

Randall also talked about competition:

> At the beginning of the movie *Patton,* Patton is standing in front of the American flag and he says, "The idea of war is not to die a hero for your country. It's to make the other poor son of a bitch die for his." When I have stiff competition and I get the sale, the thrill is not in getting the contract but in making the other poor son of a bitch not get it. It's a fight, and it isn't getting the contract that I like, it is knowing that I outsold the other guys.

Randall was aggressive, competitive, and did not waste time on niceties. Not everyone will like all of Randall's attitudes; nevertheless, as a successful businessman, he understood the value and importance of loyalty, commitment, and integrity to the long-term best interest of nonprofits and philanthropy overall. There was something ironic about Randall's observations that fund raisers should stay at their organizations longer when his own career in its early years had been marked by a number of job changes. Of course, they were within the same organization because he worked for a national agency with offices all over the country, so it was possible for him to pursue career advancement without technically leaving his employer. Yet his observation that development fails to the extent that fund raisers fail to remain in town long enough to establish personal relationships with donors is accurate and on target. However, Randall lacked compassion and insight about what to do about the problem.

Nonprofit Environment

This is a turbulent period for nonprofit organizations, a time characterized by increasingly restrictive economic conditions and severe public criticism and uncertainty. The federal government as well as some state and local governments continue to withdraw public funds from many programs in education, health care, human services, arts and culture, and other public benefit areas. While the level of public support for nonprofit organizations is a legitimate matter for public debate, the grave concern of many in the nonprofit sector is that cutbacks in public funds create an ever more urgent need for increased private funds. A complex set of factors involving organizational capacity for fund raising, as well as the limits of donors' capacity and willingness to give, will determine how well many nonprofits will be able to respond to the need to increase revenues from private sources. The complexity of this matter does not often appear to be part of the public debate about the appropriate level of public support.

A number of interviewees indicated that they experienced in their work the effects of increased competition for philanthropic funds. The increase in competition is generally related to the shift in the tax structure during the Reagan administration, which called on the nonprofit sector to assume more of the burden for social programs and a variety of government-funded programs. Several with long years of experience identified the increased competition as the most significant change in fund-raising practice they had experienced. A veteran fund raiser said he realized that competition had increased dramatically when he met a development officer with a staff of twelve who managed a sophisticated fund-raising program for a public high school. We are indebted to one of the anonymous reviewers of a draft of this manuscript who supplied the example of a government employee with the title "revenue enhancement manager" who was enrolled in a university-based program in fund raising. This person, whose tuition was paid by county funds, was in training to seek private support to replace diminished tax dollars for some government programs.

Although we do not know exactly how many people work full time as fund raisers, we do know that membership in fund-raising professional organizations has dramatically increased. For instance, NSFRE membership increased from 2,913 in 1981 to over 16,000 in 1995. The number of 501(c)(3) organizations more than doubled from 279,895 in 1983 (Internal Revenue Service, 1987) to 575,690 in 1993 (Kaplan, 1995). During this time, new community foundations grew at a rapid rate, increasing from 208 in 1981 to 374 in 1993 (Council on Foundations, 1994), and those with assets of at least $1 million or grants programs of at least $100,000 increased 250 percent from 98 to 269 (Renz, Lawrence, and Treiber, 1995).

Community foundations were a response to local needs for increased funding and the availability of increased personal assets in the $2–$10 million range made possible by tax changes during the Reagan administration. Community foundations assist donors who may not have the level of assets to establish a private foundation. Some fund raisers seek ways to cooperate with community foundations to develop funding for their programs. Others see community foundations as another source of competition. Some interviewees indicated that a weak economy during the early part of the decade added to the challenge of competition. There were dramatic decreases in corporate giving and major changes in strategies governing corporate charitable contributions. Overall, there are more organizations with more full-time fund raisers seeking more funds that are more difficult for donors to give.

Most people still say their reason for not giving is that they were not asked, so increased competition for philanthropic dollars by a larger force of professional fund raisers should theoretically help expand the total amount of philanthropic funds available; fund raisers refer to this as "enlarging the pie." However, although total philanthropic dollars have increased, their portion of the Gross Domestic Product (GDP) has remained stable for more than thirty years. As reported in *Giving USA 1994* (Kaplan, 1994), in 1963, philanthropic giving in the United States amounted to $13 billion, 2.2 percent of the GDP. In 1983 and 1993 respectively, giving amounted roughly to $63 billion and $126 billion, representing 1.9 percent and 2 percent of the GDP. Several interviewees were disturbed and puzzled by this phenomenon. It is possible that the increased investment in asking has been necessary to maintain the constant 2 percent of GDP. It is also possible that there has not been enough time since the growth of fund-raising efforts to realize dramatic increases in major and planned gifts. Ultimately, the fund-raising field will be held accountable for the level of philanthropic support in this country. Because of the increased investment in fund-raising programs and personnel, nonprofit organizations, as well as watchdog and regulatory agencies, will expect to see increases in philanthropy as a percentage of the GDP.

Also as indicated elsewhere, nonprofits have attempted to follow exhortations to become more businesslike—and now many see that as part of the problem nonprofits have to deal with today. One interviewee said:

> I think we have to return to a mission-driven approach to philanthropy. In health care, for instance, in the 1980s we adopted the language of marketing and business and we started talking about the bottom line and market share. If we talk to corporate officers in the same language they use to talk to their shareholders, it reinforces the notion that we are another business, and asking for a donation makes as much sense as asking for a contribution for K-Mart.

Other subsectors have other dilemmas. Every interviewee who worked in fund raising for the arts spoke of the difficulty in articulating a convincing case for support of the arts when problems of the poor, the homeless, and those with AIDS are so central in the public awareness. Higher education fund raisers spoke of the increased challenge to make the case for colleges and universities when many donors, particularly foundation and corporate donors, are increasingly concerned about lower educational standards and student outcomes in elementary and secondary schools.

Entry and Advancement

How people prepare to become fund raisers and enter and advance in the field raise a series of critical issues that are closely related. We indicated earlier that most fund raisers today are college educated and an increasing number have graduate and professional degrees, and that their educational backgrounds vary widely. However, the only consensus about education among fund raisers is that fund raisers should be educated—there is no consensus in the field about what constitutes the best educational preparation for fund raising.

Preparation for Fund Raising

Some fund raisers favor professional education in fund raising, some favor professional education in some other field, such as business or social work, and some advocate a broad liberal arts education. Interviewees with education or previous experience in teaching, educational administration, arts management, other nonprofit management, law, banking, public relations, the modeling industry, and the clergy all said that work in these fields was excellent preparation for a career in fund raising. Some interviewees stated that the content knowledge they acquired in those fields helped them in fund raising but most of them indicated that the skills and understanding developed in previous jobs were most useful in their fund-raising careers. Most of all, they emphasized skills in interpersonal relationships and experience in working with a wide range of people.

One chief development officer said that fund raising is a good place for people making a midcareer change. In his large operation, he sought to hire people who had worked in other fields, especially if they worked extensively with a variety of types of people. He was not particularly interested in hiring people with fund-raising experience, saying, "If fund raisers who are in the market are so good, why are they available?" By contrast, another interviewee said he had observed that people who came to fund raising after significant experience in another field often assumed they knew more than they did and made costly mistakes. These different perceptions highlight the range of reasoned views about preparation for entry to the field. They also reflect the essence of the conflict about whether fund raising is or can ever be a profession. It is not conceivable that someone needing to hire a physician would prefer candidates who had worked in some other field rather than those with specific training and experience in medicine.

A final area regarding issues related to entering and advancing in the fund-raising field is an issue for almost all fields and involves the promotion of practitioners to higher-paying, more responsible management positions. In every field, the best practitioners—the best doctors, teachers, radiology technologists, accountants, and fund raisers—are tapped for promotions to management positions where the required skills may be very different from and in some cases conflict with the skills that made them the best practitioners. This is an especially critical issue in fund raising because so much of the transfer of knowledge in the field is informal and dependent upon more experienced practitioners passing on their knowledge and the benefits of their experience to newcomers.

Certification and Licensing

Currently, many discussions about qualifications for fund raising center around the issues of certification and licensing of fund raisers. If there is no consensus about appropriate educational preparation, there is even less agreement regarding certification and licensing. Many fund raisers are concerned that anyone can call herself or himself a fund raiser. Some believe the lack of entry standards contribute both to the poor self-image among fund raisers and to the public's negative image of fund raisers. Others are concerned that those with inadequate knowledge and experience and insufficient understanding of ethical issues make serious mistakes that reflect on the field generally.

Certification generally implies that professional organizations provide credentials for members who demonstrate a certain level of knowledge and experience and subscribe to a code of ethics and acceptable practice. AHP and NSFRE both have programs to certify fund raisers. Procedures, requirements, and goals of the two programs are similar. Both programs offer two levels of certification, one for members with five years' experience in the field, and an advanced level for those with eight years (AHP) or ten years (NSFRE) in the field.

Both programs require applicants to score a minimum number of points for formal and continuing education, breadth of experience, specific accomplishments, and service to the professional organization or society, and both programs require applicants to pass a written examination designed to test fund-raising knowledge. Also, both programs require applicants to agree in writing to uphold the sponsoring organization's code of ethics. In general, the goals of the two programs are to support professional development of members, to recognize the professional achievement of members, and to provide a guideline for professional standards to employing organizations.

NSFRE and AHP officials are currently engaged in discussions about the possibility of programs to provide joint basic certification. Currently, about 25 percent of members in each organization are certified. If certified members fail to continue to meet certification requirements, certification can be removed. One aspect in the success of voluntary certification depends on the value employing organizations place on the certification. One national leader in fund raising said he did not know of one organization that currently selects fund raisers solely on the basis of certification. Clearly, many more nonprofit executives need to be educated about certification before it can become widespread or meaningful as a credential in employment. There is a core of thoughtful people in both organizations dedicated to the continual evaluation and review of certification programs, people who are well aware of the criticisms of current programs.

The proponents of certification argue that although monitoring and enforcing standards are complex processes, the certification procedures represent a good beginning. Proponents usually also argue that fund raisers had better regulate themselves to ward off regulation by outside groups. One interviewee said:

> Certification has meant an awful lot to people in the field. If nothing else, it demonstrates a commitment to the field and the fact that those certified have been exposed to the basic elements of fund raising, but it doesn't mean a person is any more or less skilled or effective. It is important that it not be misunderstood.

Others indicated that existing certification programs lack validity. One said:

> The certification programs are a total scam and have really turned me off. They may have some noble purposes but I don't think they pull them off. I know people who have certification who don't know what they're doing. Certification is a half-baked attempt to professionalize the field, but it's not working.

Another interviewee said:

> A lot of people with certification spend all their time working for the professional organization rather than for the profession and they don't always know what they're talking about. I've gotten wrong information from people represented as experts. I remember one certified fund raiser presenting at a conference who said the future of philanthropy was in matching gifts—at the very time that matching gifts programs were being dismantled at major companies all over the country!

Licensing generally refers to a formal, legal, state, or local process that regulates preparation for and entry into a field, such as is currently in place for doctors, lawyers, nurses, real estate salespersons, accountants, and others. No such laws regarding fund raisers currently exist, although there are a variety of state laws now regulating fund-raising activity, particularly those activities conducted by persons who are not staff members of nonprofit organizations.

The proponents of licensing argue that only through the power of legal regulation can the public be assured that unethical behavior will be dealt with forthrightly. Proponents also argue that if fund raisers cannot pass muster through legal regulation, they lose credibility with the public.

Critics of licensing argue that enforcement would be impossible given current state resources and that the system would still have to rely on fund raisers to monitor each other. Additionally, there are pragmatic questions about who would require licensing. For instance, if a CEO spends 30 percent or 50 percent of work time on fund raising, would the CEO be required to be licensed as a fund raiser? If a fund raiser had other related duties, at what level would no license be required?

Legal scholars who are experts in the nonprofit sector believe fund raisers do not take self-regulation and the possibility of increased external regulation seriously enough. Hopkins (1996) wrote, "The fund raising community is generally engaging in classic denial in relation to government regulation of its practices" (p. xii). He indicated that this attitude is potentially harmful because of the extensive regulations across states with which fund raisers must cope. Without the active engagement of fund raisers in the development of regulations, uninformed lawmakers may cause harm to philanthropy while trying to protect it. Dale (1991) said that if fund raisers do not take self-regulation seriously and develop a means of enforcement, the result will be regulation by state and local governments that may not be in the long-term best interests of philanthropy or those working in fund raising.

Women and Minorities in Fund Raising

All the research to date, including this study, indicates that significant sexism and even more significant racism operate in the fund-raising field. This is not to say that fund raisers as individuals are sexist and racist, but the fund-raising field clearly reflects the sexism and racism prevalent in American society and especially in the nonprofit sector today. As with self-regulation, these do not appear to be issues that most fund raisers take very seriously.

Diversity issues have attracted the attention of for-profit organizations because it has been demonstrated that failure to diversify the workforce will have an increasingly serious and negative impact on the bottom line. Research has indicated that there will continue to be more women and minorities in the workforce and far fewer white males. How will a much more diversified workforce affect the work of fund raising? Perhaps there has not been enough visionary thinking about what impact the failure to diversify the fund-raising workforce and to eliminate gender-based salary and position disparities will have on the bottom line. Fund raisers are forewarned by experience of other fields that if a field becomes feminized, that is, begins to be seen as women's work, that field will decline in status and its overall salary levels will be driven down. There is compelling evidence that these consequences will not enhance the fund-raising field.

In relation to the lack of ethnic diversity, one national leader in fund raising observed that the field has not actively participated in the aggressive competition for talented minorities and has not made systematic efforts to demonstrate that fund raising can provide attractive career opportunities for minorities. An organization that now functions effectively with a nondiversified workforce will have to make adjustments to function effectively with a diversified workforce. Visionary thinkers in the for-profit sector have determined that those organizations that are proactive in recruiting minorities and making requisite adjustments will have the edge in competing for minority applicants. Simply put, the most capable minority applicants will seek out organizations with the strongest records of providing hospitable environments for minorities.

In addition to factors related to overall efficiency and effectiveness, there are significant values underlying equity in hiring and compensation. Because these issues involve basic elements of justice and integrity, the nonprofit sector should provide leadership in these areas. Independent Sector (1991) argues that nonprofit organizations have an obligation to live beyond the law, to provide an example, and to demonstrate higher standards than other organizations in our society. By providing leadership in diversity, the nonprofit sector can better fulfill its obligation to the public by demonstrating leadership on one of America's most fundamental and critical problems.

Turnover in Fund Raising

A critical issue identified by many survey respondents and interviewees was the amount of turnover in fund raising. As we indicated in Chapter Three, our study demonstrates that turnover is less of a problem than it might have been a decade ago and also is less of a problem than many fund raisers believe it is. We found that the average tenure for all female respondents was 3.31 years and for all male respondents was 4.42, but that average tenure increased for those with ten or more years' experience to 4.6 years for women and 5.72 years for men.

Among those who saw turnover as a problem, some attributed it to excessive self-interest on the part of fund raisers. Others, including the interviewee quoted in Chapter Four who described someone who "parlays one year of experience twenty times as twenty years experience," suggested that the fund-raising field was too tolerant of turnover. Nevertheless, there are fund raisers who consistently demonstrate higher values. One interviewee told of her experience of being recruited to another position:

> Someone called me from another college. I don't even know how they got my name. I went to talk and, boy, the money was fabulous but I couldn't get excited about that place if they put a firecracker under me. I even tried to get excited because the salary was really good, but—nothing. I knew this would not be in my best interest, it wouldn't be in the school's best interest, and I turned it down.

Without a mission to energize this fund raiser, the salary was not sufficient to cause her to change positions. This behavior may in fact reflect the standard to which the best fund raisers hold each other accountable.

Others attributed turnover to organizational practices. Following are typical comments:

- "I've been in this position for five years. This organization would benefit if I stayed five more years, but I would not. They will not reward me for staying."
- "Instead of paying the next guy what the market demands, organizations should create compensation programs that will encourage people to stay put."
- "The trick to retaining people is to teach them so fast that they have no motivation to go anywhere for a number of years. Teach a lot, challenge a lot, motivate a lot. Keep them too busy to look for a job."

How can we account for the difference between what the data say—that turnover is decreasing—and what fund raisers believe—that turnover is excessive? Some of the difference is due to the time lag in perceptions from the period of a decade or more ago when growth and turnover were higher. Part of the problem is that most fund raisers know or know of people who have made rapid job changes, and anyone who screens résumés for fund-raising jobs sees the evidence that some fund raisers change jobs frequently. Fund raisers who move from job to job to improve their salaries and professional standing are perceived by other fund raisers and the public to reflect excessive self-interest in a field that promotes concern for others as one of its highest values. For some fund raisers, the issue of commitment to the cause, to the organization, is such a critical element that even moderate rates of turnover are problematic, but it is essential that fund raisers can have the opportunity for career advancement and not be seen as purely self-serving.

Fund raisers themselves see turnover as problematic because of the strong belief that continuity and longevity of personnel are strongly related to long-term fund-raising effectiveness. Conceptually, the idea is sound, especially when considering the time line involved in major and planned gift development, but there is only anecdotal information about this phenomenon. No comprehensive research has been done to determine that fund-raising staff longevity correlates with increased success. However, if the trend toward more and more staff solicitation continues, the issue of fund-raising turnover and underlying questions about the commitment of fund raisers will become even more important. One interviewee said, "Fund raising is relationships. Volunteers used to provide the relationships. As programs become more staff-driven, long-term staff relationships with donors will have to supplant volunteer relationships."

Many survey respondents and interviewees indicated that organizations share some of the responsibility for fund-raising turnover. Organizational practices can often drive fund-raising staff away if there are unreasonable goals, if fund raisers are isolated from the rest of the organization, and if fund raisers are denied access to board members who can assist in the fund-raising process. One interviewee said:

> When the expectations of fund raisers are unrealistic, fund raisers need to be more honest about their limitations in job interviews. They need to say, "I have a good sense of your situation here," and not, "I can straighten this out or make you successful."

The expectations of fund raisers are different from the expectations of some other staff in the nonprofit and for-profit sectors. This may be one of the values fund raisers have to accept as part of their professional responsibilities.

Although it is common to read in fund-raising literature that older fund raisers express concern about the erosion of altruistic values and the increase in profit-seeking motives on the parts of those now entering the field, Harrah-Conforth and Borsos (1991) indicated that evidence exists that early fund raisers were "not immune to the quest for power and profit" (p. 23). They concluded that the tension between fund raising as a calling and fund raising as a business dates back to the earliest days of the profession (p. 19) and is "the legacy passed on by the pioneer generation" (p. 27).

Compensation

Nothing related to nonprofit organizations and their fund-raising programs has been debated publicly with as much vigor recently as the substantial compensation of some nonprofit executives, an issue with profound implications for the quality of public trust. As many have noted, it is foolish to believe that dedication to a noble cause overcomes inept management. Some nonprofits are complex organizations spending billions of dollars providing services essential to the well-being of the country. To operate efficiently and to be accountable to their publics, nonprofit organizations must be able to attract skilled and talented staff and offer challenging career paths with significant financial reward to supplement the intrinsic rewards of doing good. Nonprofit boards have the responsibility to educate the public about the need to pay salaries that attract talented staff. In addition, those who staff nonprofit organizations are entrusted with using resources wisely for the public good. If nonprofit executives are to be good stewards of public resources, they must engage in public dialogue about how those funds are being used. Nonprofit executives must support the need for both disclosure of salary levels and adequate compensation if the nonprofit sector is to continue to fulfill its role.

Fund raisers are in close contact with volunteers and donors who have expectations about how their funds are being used. They hear first-hand the resentment expressed about nonprofit salaries and they have the opportunity to help educate volunteers and donors about the costs of operating nonprofits effectively, about how overall nonprofit compensation levels compare to for-profit salaries, and about the fact that most nonprofit salaries, including those of most nonprofit executives, are modest.

Another issue related to compensation in fund raising involves paying fund raisers based on commission or a percentage of funds raised.

The codes of ethics for AHP, CASE, NSFRE, and AAFRC ask members to make a commitment to accept pay only on a salary or fee-for-service basis. The codes ask members in good standing not to accept payment on a commission basis. Yet several of these organizations eliminated the prohibition against percentage-based compensation for a few years because of fear of being sued under antitrust regulations by fund raisers interested both in being compensated on a percentage basis and in enjoying the status and credibility that membership in a professional organization provides. Most practitioners were pleased to see the prohibition against percentage compensation restored to the codes of ethics. Nevertheless, in spite of the codes and the widespread opinion in the field that percentage compensation is harmful to the field, the pressure to consider percentage compensation continues in some organizations, often promoted by members of governing boards accustomed to using percentage-based compensation as an incentive for motivating their own sales forces in for-profit organizations.

Many fund raisers believe that percentage-based compensation jeopardizes the future of philanthropy, and those interviewed for this study generally agreed. First, fund raisers are put in the position of placing their interests ahead of the interests of donors when compensation depends on short-term gain. Second, the interest of the organization may not be well served by percentage compensation. If long-term organizational fund-raising success depends upon long-term involvement of constituents and donors with nonprofit organizations, then percentage compensation based on current income may jeopardize future major gifts. Third, because much of fund-raising income is the result of long-term relationships and even serendipity, providing compensation based on current income sometimes rewards fund raisers for work they did not do.

As Bok (1993) noted, more emphasis on rewards leads to more temptation to violate rules, in this case, translated as violating the rules of donor interest. One interviewee said:

> I believe in institutional or departmental goals, but I don't agree with putting a dollar goal on what individual fund raisers must raise each year. I know of a planned giving officer who was told that he had to get in writing $5 million worth of will commitments this year. This poor guy is in an impossible bind. Is he going to lie or inflate? He's tempted to. Some schools are paying bonuses on productivity. How do you do that? One year we got a check for an $11 million estate settlement that nobody knew about. Who would get the bonus for that gift? It's usually trustees coming out of a company environment that recommend bonuses for performance. I think it encourages dishonesty.

Perhaps the strongest argument against percentage-based compensation is the nondistribution clause of the 501(c)(3) code. This code, which defines how organizations qualify for charitable gift deductions, states in part that no surpluses that an organization realizes may enure to anyone involved with the organization. Percentage-based compensation creates the perception that part of each contribution goes directly to the fund raiser. For this and the reasons cited earlier, most fund raisers in our study supported the practice of compensation as salary or fee-for-service.

The NSFRE's standards of professional practice (National Society of Fund Raising Executives, 1995) allow for bonuses for meritorious service or for meeting or exceeding established goals, provided that all employees in the organization are paid on the same bonus system. Other professional codes are silent on the bonus issue. However, even bonus pay is not universally accepted. Some fund raisers fear that approving bonus pay is the first step in approving percentage-based compensation.

The final matter concerning compensation is the disparity in salaries for men and women in fund raising, which ought to be of equal interest to both men and women, and to the organizations that employ them. As a matter of justice, women should be compensated at the same level as men when they bring similar skills and backgrounds to similar jobs. From a practical standpoint, all fund raisers will eventually earn less if feminization of the field takes place. All nonprofit organizations will be affected because it will become more and more difficult to keep good people in critical fund-raising positions.

Women must take responsibility for becoming more knowledgeable about competitive salaries and about what they should expect to earn based on experience, education, geographic region, and type of organization. They must be cautious of exploitation when moving from volunteer to paid positions and from part-time to full-time status. Those who hire fund raisers must make ethical commitments to gender-blind employment. Nonprofit organizations, beginning at the level of boards of trustees, must develop and put in place policies that ensure justice and equality between men and women. The integrity of the nonprofit sector and the fund-raising field depends on ending the disparity in compensation for men and women. Again, as indicated earlier, this is an opportunity for the nonprofit sector to provide leadership for the public good by eliminating gender disparity in compensation.

Perceptions Inside and Outside the Field

The lack of understanding among the public about fund raising is compounded by the varied forms of fund raising the public encounters, many of which seem both irritating and self-serving. In the face of this confusion, negative perceptions of fund raising are easy to form and difficult to dispel, and both nonprofit management and fund raisers themselves sometimes share these perceptions.

Lack of Understanding

As far as the public is concerned, fund raising includes everything that involves asking for money. Fund raisers are the ones who make those cold telephone calls during the dinner hour to prospects they've never met and the ones who grind out the direct mail pieces that fill the public's mailboxes. They are also the people behind the candy sales at local elementary schools, the silent auctions by arts organizations, and the golf outings that generate funds for minority scholarships. At the same time, local pastors asking parishioners to establish million-dollar trust funds for the church are fund raisers, and so are the people organizing university campaigns with billion-dollar targets. In all this, there is little opportunity to engage the public in a discussion of the rationale for a total development program in which many different activities at multiple levels support the continued involvement of various constituents.

Despite the prevalence of a lack of understanding of the fund-raising process by the public, fund raisers are not as affected by ignorance in that quarter as they are by the lack of understanding of the fund-raising process by CEOs, board members, and other key organizational members. Respondents acknowledged this lack of understanding as one of the major problems they face. This lack of understanding most often manifests itself in the failure or reluctance of boards and CEOs to participate directly in fund raising, but the lack of understanding also limits the ability of the board and CEO to evaluate the effectiveness or efficiency of their organizations' fund-raising programs.

One interviewee summarized the problem this way: "There are CEOs who just don't have a clue, and it does make it hard for fund raisers." A few indicated they worked for CEOs who understood and were supportive of fund-raising efforts, but most reported problems with CEOs. One interviewee noted, "It always filters down to 'What have you done for me today?'" This comment suggests another common problem, that CEOs and boards often remove themselves from any responsibility for participating in fund-raising activities. Fund raisers may be left with goals set by CEOs and trustees that do indeed reflect organizational needs but may not at all reflect fund-raising capacity. Moreover, fund raisers are expected in many cases to meet these unrealistic goals isolated from the program staff, administration, and board members who provide the necessary linkages to the organization's donor constituencies. Hank Rosso, the founder and director emeritus of The Fund Raising School, indicated that the most common problem participants at the school report is that they can't get their CEO or their boards involved in fund raising (1991, p. 133).

Many believe the answer lies in educating boards and CEOs about fund raising, but fund raisers also know that this proposed solution is difficult to implement. Offering appropriate seminars and conferences is a straightforward solution, but experience indicates that CEOs and board members often will not take the time to attend such programs. This usually means that fund raisers are left with the burden of educating their own boards and CEOs.

Many interviewees were skeptical or discouraged about their ability to educate CEOs and others. One interviewee noted that her CEO "says the weirdest things to people" in fund-raising situations. She said she previously tried to educate him regarding fund raising, but she decided she was "not responsible for turning this social worker into an administrator and fund raiser." She said that her dream was to work for an administrator who was a former fund raiser. Another interviewee explained that she reported to a vice president who not only did not understand fund raising but who was also cynical about fund raising. This vice president equated securing private gifts with "putting the squeeze on" prospective donors. This interviewee said she was tired of educating her bosses and would eventually seek a position "in an organization with a more sophisticated, more enlightened" stance toward fund raising. These comments from interviewees reflect the tension fund raisers feel about this challenge. They are frustrated by the lack of understanding of their work, and many have no authority to "manage up" in such a way as to secure the involvement and ensure the edification of the CEO and board. This clearly is a critical factor for continuing education for fund raisers, who need help in developing the skills to be effective in this role.

Other interviewees referred to other indications that fund raising is not well understood, as the following comments indicate:

- "Fund raising is not the answer to all the organization's problems. When I came here, the feeling was 'Development can't do anything.' Well, we did do some things they said we couldn't do, so now they say, 'Development can do everything.' I have to go to board meetings and say, 'These are the things we can do now, and these are the things we can do after that, and there are some things we aren't ever going to be able to do.' Organizations need to have more realistic expectations and fund raisers need to be more honest about what they can accomplish."
- "When they want to fire a coach, the president tries to assign him to development. Development chiefs need to be able to say no, that will hurt my operations, and I won't have it."

Negative Public Perception

A critical issue requiring attention is the general negative perception of fund raisers. One interviewee said, "When fund raisers walk in, people say, 'You better watch your wallet.'" Many other interviewees mentioned having experienced negative reactions from others as a result of working in fund raising, as the following indicate:

- "People have said to me, 'Who are you hitting up today? Whose money are you spending today?' The ones who say these things are often people of means who don't want to share what they have."
- "I've been called a pickpocket. Fund raising is still a dirty word for some, and the negative perception may never be overcome because some people don't want to give and so they blame fund raisers."
- "Often the reaction I get when I say I work in fund raising is aversion. Once people understand that I am not going to wrestle them to the ground to get their money, they start to appreciate what I do."
- "At a barbecue for new employees at the president's house, I was sitting with the provost who didn't know I was in development. He said development people are like a bunch of used car salesmen, but the difference was that typically the used car salesmen were nice people and that made you want to buy the car."

- "People actually think my job is to sit on the phone all day, calling and bugging people. We don't get $10,000 gifts by calling people up and bugging them at dinner time."
- "I have dear friends who have physically recoiled when I said I was paid to fund raise—either that or they say they themselves couldn't do such a hard job. There is such a taboo about talking about money."
- "Our status is low, mostly because of charlatans. It is disheartening, particularly when it comes from those who should know better. I recently met a priest who referred to fund raisers as a necessary evil—this, from someone whose whole career has depended on the philanthropy of his parishioners."
- "People back off when they find out I am a fund raiser, but I try to explain that I am working for important causes and working mostly with people who really want to contribute."
- "I take faculty members on calls. They love getting the gift but in their minds, I'm the sleazy salesman who asks for the money while they get to be the noble scholars who are pained by the whole process."

Many respondents indicated that their acceptance as valued colleagues in their host organizations is not very high, even though there are high expectations that fund raisers will exhibit strong organizational commitment. Many reported that unflattering stereotypes still prevail. Nevertheless, some other interviewees thought the negative perception of fund raisers is changing, as the following comments indicate:

- "Fund raisers are integral now. Faculty used to put up with them but would not invite them for dinner. The faculty now consider fund raisers as colleagues, which is a real change."
- "Fund raisers are no longer held in low esteem by educated, knowledgeable persons. If a development officer is not well received by the faculty, it's probably the development officer's problem."
- "Years ago, I didn't want to tell people I was a fund raiser because we were looked down upon. Now I'm comfortable saying I am a fund raiser because, through our professional organizations, the public that matters—corporate and foundation executives, community relations people, key volunteers—

> see us as professionals and respect us. In fact, I think they
> like us—a big difference from years ago. I no longer feel sub-
> servient to these people; I feel on a par with them."

Although some may indicate that the negative image of fund
raisers is improving, there are also reasons to think that the image
of fund raising may actually be deteriorating. There are now forty-
five states with laws that require registration or regulation of nonprofit organizations or fund-raising activity. Many of these statutes
are the result of activity that violated local community standards of
acceptable fund-raising behavior or fund-raising costs. Many differentiate between paid staff and volunteers who solicit on behalf
of their organizations and paid consultants and solicitors, who
often must register and often are not permitted to accept gifts on
behalf of the organization. These statutes reflect general great dis-
trust of fund raisers among the public and their elected officials.

However, there is evidence that fund raisers are valued by volunteers who raise money. Seiler and Tempel (1994) reported that
volunteers value the organizational skills and expertise that fund
raisers bring to the process. Trustees especially noted paid fund
raisers' expertise in the management of the fund-raising process
and their ethical perspectives, respect for donors, and knowledge
of volunteer management, the community, the prospect research
process, and the organization's programs. Trustees also valued
fund raisers for their organizational skills, strategic thinking skills,
enthusiasm, pride in the work they do, and detail management
skills. Trustees who were successfully engaged in fund-raising activity and being supported by fund-raising staff had a very positive
view of fund raisers.

Education of the public about the rationale for fund-raising activity and the role that fund raising plays in the nonprofit sector
might help change public perceptions about fund raisers, but it is
overly optimistic to believe that fund raisers and their professional
organizations can adequately convey this complex message to the
public. As many fund raisers know from first-hand experience,
when a scandal is exposed, all fund-raising efforts are affected. One
interviewee said:

> There are so many dedicated fund raisers out there doing a very
> difficult job in a very difficult time with the most noble motives,

and they get no publicity for it. All of a sudden, along comes an Aramony or a Hughey and Watson, a Falwell or Bakker. Then you see negativity about fund raising in the newspapers, and everybody thinks that fund raisers are slime. They're not. For the most part, fund raisers do a hell of a difficult job under terribly difficult conditions, they're not well paid, and they provide essential resources to organizations that are helping people.

There will not soon be a major change in public perceptions of fund raisers. Fund raisers must start with improving their image internally—a significant problem, given the amount of negative feelings among those in the field about fund raisers and fund raising.

Fund Raisers' Negative Feelings About Fund Raising

One of the most serious challenges facing fund raisers and hampering the professionalization of fund raising as a field is the discomfort with and distaste for fund raising experienced by fund raisers themselves. Discovering that fund raisers believe that important constituencies have negative perceptions of fund raisers was no surprise. What was a surprise was the realization that many fund raisers themselves have a negative perception of fund raisers and the field in general. Although all the research participants knew other fund raisers they respected and whom they believed demonstrated what the ideal fund raiser should be like, many participants also made strong negative judgments about other fund raisers and the field of fund raising. One interviewee said:

> I recently met a person who has been in the field for ten years who said he still doesn't know how to talk to people about his work. He doesn't feel comfortable after all these years and doesn't know how to make a statement about what he does that conveys pride and honor.

Many fund raisers interviewed for this study mentioned that they themselves had negative opinions about fund raising at some time in the past. Their perceptions were changed through understanding of and involvement in the fund-raising process. For many others, however, the negative feelings continue. This research indicated that negative feelings among fund raisers were of two kinds. One group of fund raisers had strong negative feelings about staff solicitations or about being solicitors themselves. Another group of fund raisers, similar to the public generally, seemed to have overall negative feelings about the fund-raising field and saw themselves and perhaps the few good fund raisers they knew as exceptions to the rule.

Negative Feelings About Direct Solicitation

In several places throughout this book, we referred to the way staff solicitation has replaced volunteer solicitation in many organizations. For some, the practice of staff solicitation is a violation of one of the most elemental factors in classic fund raising—that of peers soliciting peers, people of affluence and influence asking others like themselves to support a particular cause. The implications for the fund-raising field of this shift is beyond the scope of this book, but how some fund raisers have reacted to this change is relevant. Many interviewees expressed discomfort about asking for money. For some, the feelings associated with asking were part of a strong conviction that peers, not paid fund raisers, are the most appropriate persons to ask for money, but for others it was discomfort with or distaste for asking, as the following comments indicate:

- "It's very hard to make myself make the call, get myself over there, push the doorbell, but once I've pushed the doorbell, the hard work is over, because as soon as the door opens, I go on automatic. I'm in my element and that's pure joy."
- "I don't think I could ever ask for money. I didn't grow up in a well-to-do family and I don't feel at ease with people who have money. We need to develop our capacity in this organization to do more staff solicitations, and I hope to be one of the people who put that in place but not doing it myself."
- "I'm good at cultivating but I can't make the ask. I know how to do a phonothon and a direct mail blindfolded but I can't ask."
- "I could never ask directly but I think I can help design programs to encourage people to give."
- "I am not aggressive enough. I would be petrified to go out and solicit a gift."

One interviewee said that he thought that when fund raisers get together, they should talk about this discomfort more than anything else—"that is, just what is it that makes people so uncomfortable?" He himself believes the discomfort is a matter of intimacy:

> One of the things that interests me about development work is intimacy. Money is such a powerful symbol in our culture, and when people talk about their money, they often talk about the things that are most important and closest to them. I have a sense that to do that is a more intimate involvement than we're often willing to undertake or to risk, and if you brought that up, many fund raisers might deny that. I think it is a fear of intimacy. I have made mistakes where, when I have planned in advance to ask for a specific sum, I did not, out of discomfort, do that. I don't understand this because I believe in what I'm doing, I want to do it, I know exactly what I'm supposed to say—and I don't do it.

Another interviewee, who enjoyed soliciting major gifts, nevertheless acknowledged:

> I get nervous asking for gifts. I assume everybody does. When I have to ask for a gift, I say to a colleague, "I've got to ask somebody for money tomorrow. Help me think this through, role play a little, to get prepared."

Faculty at the Fund Raising School report that participants talk freely about why people do not like to ask for money. One of the reasons often given is that they don't know how, and practicing, as suggested by this interviewee, is helpful in making fund raisers comfortable. Other reasons given include fears of rejection and of reciprocity, discomfort with assuming a subservient position as the asker, and the reluctance to pry into personal matters.

While Americans may demonstrate openly the level of financial resources they have, there are cultural taboos against discussing salary and assets openly. Asking for a gift at a certain level implies some knowledge of the person's income and assets. It may be a lack of intimacy in the personal relationship that causes the tension in the asking process.

Our research indicated that a commitment to the organization was a key factor in finding satisfaction in a fund-raising career.

Perhaps commitment is also a key factor in finding comfort in asking for money. Commitment to the organization becomes the key motivation for asking. If fund raisers ask or arrange for volunteers to ask only through applying fund-raising skills but without the underlying commitment, the potential for discomfort and distaste increases. Open discussion of the issues surrounding discomfort and distaste for fund raising, training in fund-raising techniques, opportunities to broaden fund raisers' knowledge about philanthropy, mentorships for less experienced staff, and opportunities for renewal are important professional requirements to deal with this challenge.

Negative Feelings About Other Fund Raisers

Overall, there was a surprising amount of negative feeling about other fund raisers expressed by survey respondents and interviewees. Some representative comments are:

- "There are too many fund raisers hung up on titles, offices, and reporting relationships, and talking too much about what they've done. Fund raisers who say they have to be part of the top management team are just looking for self-aggrandizement and for excuses not to be out there raising money."
- "People who move around in development must have a different reason for being in fund raising than I have. We have in common that we are development officers, but beyond that I have to search to find what else we have in common. I've known a lot of people who have been fund raisers and there are few for whom I have a very high regard."
- "I just marvel at how self-important some fund raisers are."
- "I've run into too many fund raisers, especially at conferences, who talk big but don't know what they're doing."
- "A lot of the people who write articles and give classes don't know what they're doing, but they know how to write articles and give classes."
- "I really resent fund raisers who worry about having an autopen so the signature doesn't smudge but who don't worry about how long it takes to get the thank-you letter in the mail. These are the same fund raisers who know the language and

the techniques but don't know a damn thing about working till eleven-thirty at night to get that proposal or follow-up report done."

There is also some concern that younger fund raisers may not be approaching fund raising from the same value base and for the same rewards that more mature fund raisers did:

> In my generation, we probably went too far in the direction of investing in work and not enough time with our families. I know it hurt my first marriage. Today I find a lot of development officers who are not willing to work as hard, not as willing to put in the hours, and who are more reluctant to take risks. They are more focused on "I raised," rather than "we raised." This is a disturbing trend and I am worried about the work habits of a lot of the people who work in the field now. People look at their watches and get up and go home at five o'clock. This was unheard of ten to fifteen years ago among people who were serious about this work.

In addition to affecting individual fund raisers, this widespread negative perception of the field has serious implications. This negative perception surely affects how people choose the field, the kinds of people attracted to the field, and the whole environment in which fund raisers work. Failure to take this issue seriously and to face it directly results in missed opportunities to examine negative perceptions and reactions for whatever truths may be present, to support fund raisers in dealing with their own feelings and the negative reactions of others, and perhaps most important, to refute the inappropriate stereotypes.

Fund raisers must start with improving the image of fund raisers internally. Developing a positive self-image based on the good that is accomplished, insisting on ethical behavior from colleagues, and above all, explaining the work with pride and confidence, are the most important steps. The many fund raisers who are respected and valued in their organizations and communities can take note of the ways in which they unwittingly contribute to the persistence of widespread negative images of fund raisers and the ways in which they allow the negative images to go unchallenged. In the long run, it does not benefit well-regarded fund raisers, their organizations, or the fund-raising field if the ones who consider themselves the good ones dissociate themselves from the field.

Accountability and Ethics

The final critical issue is another complex one, somewhat inadequately labeled "accountability and ethics," but perhaps better called "telling the truth in fund raising." This critical issue does not directly concern ethics in fund raising, which is a complex and important area beyond the scope of this research. The issue under consideration here relates more to aspects of the field that verge on being or affecting ethical matters, and as a result contribute to the misunderstanding and negative perceptions of the field.

Telling the Truth About Results

The first topic concerns the lack of standards for counting and reporting gifts. Many interviewees and survey respondents indicated that the lack of uniform standards for counting and reporting gifts is a serious issue with far-reaching implications for fund-raising practice and particularly for how the field is perceived. It is also one of the factors that make it possible for those who wish to do so to deliberately misrepresent results. Although all the codes of ethics of the professional organizations include statements on accuracy in reporting gift totals, and although CASE has recently published standards for campaign reporting (born out of a long, contentious process involving considerable input from practicing fund raisers), these standards are often viewed as voluntary guidelines. As long as uniform standards are not in wide use, fund raisers will always be vulnerable to claims of misrepresentation and those intending to deceive or misrepresent will have ample opportunities to do so.

Telling the Truth About Relationships

One of the reasons telling the whole truth in fund raising is sometimes difficult is because of the pervasive question about whether fund raising is a mission or a business. Perhaps the most illuminating example of this came in an interview with one of the most introspective, thoughtful people in the entire group of interviewees, an indisputably honorable man. At this point in the interview, we were discussing the art and science of fund raising. After the interviewee explained that he thought the art of fund raising derived from a deep commitment to the organization coupled with a genuine regard for people, he began talking about a new staff member he had just hired who was inexperienced in fund raising. That portion of the actual interview follows:

Interviewee: So when she went to talk to Mrs. Jones, a very wealthy woman, she had a context for doing that, but she knew she was not going to get a gift. The woman said to her, "What do you want, Maryann?" Maryann said, "I don't want anything. My grandmother mentioned you and said I would enjoy meeting you, so I thought I would come talk to you." The woman said, "Do you want to talk to me about the college?" Maryann said, "Well, we could, but I just wanted to meet you." This is a woman we should have been visiting on a regular basis twenty years ago. Maybe it's too late because she is now eighty-seven years old. But what's important here is that Maryann may be weak on the science part, but she's good at—

Interviewer: But wasn't Maryann being disingenuous?

Interviewee: Do you mean dishonest?

Interviewer: Well, maybe.

Interviewee: No. No. If you knew Maryann, you would know she was very sincere.

Interviewer: But the college does want something from this lady?

Interviewee: Not at that visit. Maryann was honest when she said she wanted to get to know her. That was true.

Interviewer: Yes, I'm sure, but was it the whole truth? I mean, wasn't her intention in developing this relationship to ultimately ask for a gift? I mean, you said maybe it's too late—

Interviewee: Yes, I think it is in that case—but Maryann has to learn the science, too, and I have to push her on that. . . .

The interviewee's changing the subject helped to make this a particularly poignant moment. The interviewee was uncomfortable about acknowledging that Maryann was visiting this prospect to determine if she might be cultivated for a major gift. One of the ways in which the pervasive question about the conflict between fund raising as mission or as business manifests itself is in how hard it is for some fund raisers—perhaps especially those who genuinely do care about both their organizations and the people who provide support to their organizations—to admit that the relationship is important because the organization wants something from the prospect. The experienced fund raiser in this interview knew that Maryann was not visiting the elderly woman only because she wanted to meet her. The fund raiser also knew that Maryann was using her grandmother's relationship with the prospect to get to know the prospect better. What was poignant about this moment in the interview was not that there is anything either unusual or immoral about this kind of transaction in fund raising, but that the interviewee felt awkward and defensive. The quintessential feature of fund raising is the forming of relationships with people in order to persuade them to become donors. For some fund raisers, even the good ones, there are times when that is just hard to admit.

Telling the Truth About Fund-Raising Costs

Although most interviewees did not mention fund-raising costs, there were a few who were concerned about this issue, as the following comments indicate:

- "I think fund raisers as a whole should be more honest about costs. Fund raising is expensive and fund raisers don't want people to know that because people don't want to know that forty cents of their dollar is going to pay for the fund-raising effort. Many organizations include strange kinds of gifts in the bottom line so the fund-raising costs look lower. Then that artificially lowered cost becomes a news item and the rest of us suffer because it looks like we're spending too much."
- "Because of negative perceptions of fund raisers, fund raisers are very defensive. I think most people want to do the right thing, but it's hard to explain fund-raising costs to your board

when you know the board doesn't really understand fund raising. Even the CASE reporting standards on costs are designed to make the institution look good by not including costs related to alumni relations and publications."

Rewards

As the snapshots indicate, many fund raisers have made a long-term commitment to their work and enjoy and even love their work. The snapshots also report the kinds of rewards and satisfactions fund raisers find in their work. Certainly the majority of fund raisers found their work rewarding because they had a strong sense that they were doing good, important work that was valuable to society. Many fund raisers not only were gratified about being able to help, but they were grateful for the opportunity to do so, as some additional comments from interviewees illustrate:

- "This is the easiest job in the world. Compared to selling life insurance, this is a joy, and the world is better because of what we do."
- "I like to think that what I do brings hope to the professional staff here that we're going to have more resources, brings hope to the kids that there is help for them, and brings hope to the community that there are some solutions to these problems."
- "I could be selling used Pontiacs for a living. Or health care plans for an HMO. Fund raising is sales and I am very fortunate in the kinds of things I get to sell—causes I believe in."

Adding meaning to their lives, doing important work, and making the world better are rewards for many fund raisers, but there are other rewards as well. Our interviewees highlighted the satisfaction that can come from the importance of the work, the variety of people fund raisers meet and work with, and the sheer high of acquiring a major commitment. Comments include:

- "One of the reasons I like this job so much is that it is a job that absolutely must be done. I like being in a position that is vital. Fund raisers are among the most important people in private colleges."

- "I love one day being with clients knowing the money we raised made a difference in their lives and the next day sitting in a donor's home where the place mats cost more than my house. It is like traveling in different countries."
- "I love the access to important people. I can't imagine doing anything else. Getting a big gift can keep you going for a year. I don't know that you can get that feeling from anything else."
- "In fund raising, you meet people at the highest level of human kindness. This is a marvelous career working with good people who want to do good things."
- "It is a luxury to raise money for causes I believe in. What is great about the field is the quality of the donors and volunteers and the quality of their motivation. If we could replicate the best of the volunteer sector in the professional sector, we would be home free. I have met extraordinary people doing extraordinary things."

Some fund raisers find rewards in being effective as persuaders, motivators, negotiators, deal makers, as the following indicate:

- "The thing that turns me on about this work is taking people who are on the fence and getting them excited about what we're doing here and how they can be in on it."
- "I love the challenge of making converts—winning people over. I'll always be a fund raiser. When I die, I'll be working, I'll be fund raising."
- "I am fortunate in that I feel that this is what I was born to do. I love fund raising. I love my job. I love getting people excited. I love the random gratification that comes when that two or three people every year do something that just absolutely knocks your socks off."
- "It feels good to have people give you money. It is personally very affirming to know you were able to persuade people of means to give."

Some fund raisers found that having some success as a fund raiser is a very compelling experience. One said:

There aren't any presidents or CEOs around today who say they hate fund raising, but it used to be common. They don't say it anymore because they couldn't get the job if they felt that way. I say, either you've never done fund raising or else you've done it and failed. Because if you've ever done it and it's worked, you get hooked.

Others used expressions such as "it gets in your blood," and "it gives me a high," and "it gets under your skin" to describe how they experienced success in fund raising.

Some fund raisers found rewards in the concrete nature of the results and the accountability that comes with the numbers:

> I like the fact that fund raising is less fuzzy than some program delivery areas where it is hard to measure how you're doing. Fund raising is much more cut and dried. You either make your goal or you don't, but you know where you stand and it's easier to evaluate your own performance. I like being held accountable.

For many fund raisers, however, it is not any one of these aspects but all of them together that result in their finding so much satisfaction and reward in their work. Operating from the belief that the mission is important, they like being involved with important people, and they like the fact that their jobs involve acquiring resources. They like the competition, the excitement, the uncertainty, the risks, and the tangible signs of success. As we indicated in the first chapter, the pervasive question about fund raisers has to do with whether they are missionaries or salespeople, and the most sensible answer to that question is that the best people in the field are both.

Some fund raisers found rewards in identifying a moral basis for fund raising. One interviewee said:

> Education as an engine for democracy, as a means of providing access to this economy and to our society, is profoundly important to me. Those of us who raise money are Robin Hoods. What we're really up to is the redistribution of wealth. When someone gives this college a million dollars out of wealth accumulated from running a

textile mill on the backs of poor white Appalachians for fifty years, we have extracted money for the public good. We've gotten a gift from someone who might not be the least bit interested in what we're all about, but, for a variety of reasons, will give the gift, redeeming that money. I probably wouldn't say that publicly, but I feel that way. I think a good development officer probably lets some donors believe that philanthropy serves to support the interests of the wealthy, but I often see how money invested in this institution really works in a redemptive way. I like the Robin Hood aspects of our work.

It appears obvious that instead of being in conflict about the pervasive question of whether fund raising is a mission or a business, good fund raisers indicate that they enjoy this tension. Fund raising needs strong, educated, competent people with strong motivations and strong commitments. For this reason, those people who have strong values regarding excellence in their work, a strong desire to contribute to something beyond themselves, and a strong personal desire to be successful may be the best people working in the field. Fund raisers are principled people with strong commitments about making positive and lasting contributions to the organizations hiring them and fund raisers themselves need to be more assertive in spreading this good news. Although it will not replace the need for fund raisers to take personal responsibility, there is an ongoing need for strong leadership from employing organizations and fund-raising professional organizations. This leadership must articulate and acknowledge the need for a proper balance between the values of a mission orientation and of competitive business practices and support fund raisers in their struggles to maintain their mission orientation.

Chapter Nine

Building on Fund-Raising Research

This study was designed to build a stronger base of knowledge about the people who work as fund raisers. We wanted to know how they came to fund raising, what skills, abilities, and values they have, and how they feel about what they do, as well as about the fund-raising field. What we learned has implications for fund raisers themselves, for fund-raising leaders (both within and outside the professional organizations serving fund raisers), and for nonprofit leaders who hire and depend on fund raisers. This study was also designed, in part, to help researchers learn more about how to study fund raisers. What we learned leads to recommendations for additional research.

Implications for Fund Raisers

The strength of the fund-raising field is rooted in the high level of education of fund raisers, their personal commitments to philanthropy, to their organizations, and to the field of fund raising, and the passion and zest they have for the work. We are optimistic that the practice of fund raising will continue to become more professional as the field and its professional organizations become more mature. Nevertheless, fund raisers are still not generally well regarded. As one interviewee noted, he himself once believed that a person could not ask others for money and still be a "nice person." The essential tension of fund raising as a business and fund raising as a mission (Harrah-Conforth and Borsos, 1991) creates a negative connotation of the work for many people, some of whom, fund raisers note, ought to know better.

Because of this tension and the added fact that fund-raising success is perceived as a developmental process, fund raisers are often judged by others on the strength of their commitment to their organizations, as demonstrated by their job histories. They may be held to standards of less freedom of mobility than others in the nonprofit sector; as they seek career advancement, they risk being labeled as opportunistic. In many other industries, there is an acknowledged place for new venture managers—those whose strengths lie in their ability to conceive and implement new programs. In many cases, new venture managers are not the people best suited to long-term management. There is a need for new venture managers in fund raising, and some fund raisers are particularly talented and suited for this kind of work. However, fund raisers need to be more honest about their strengths and interests and not pursue inappropriate positions to further their own careers at the expense of nonprofit organizations and important causes.

Fund raisers can all become more aware of the impact of their personal decisions and actions on the field overall. In the best interests of the field and the well-being of nonprofit organizations, fund raisers must commit themselves to a different set of standards than sales or marketing professionals in the for-profit sector. Factors other than market supply and demand should influence the career decisions they make.

Fund raisers must accept responsibility for improving the image of the field among fund raisers, other nonprofit staff, and the general public. To do this, fund raisers need to stop distancing themselves from the field and to stop presenting themselves and the other good fund raisers they know as exceptions to the rule. The truth about the strength and character of the majority of fund raisers needs to be told, and the telling must start within the field. Fund raisers must also be scrupulously honest in their job searches and in how they present themselves to prospective employers. They can also help to advance the mission and work of fund raisers' professional organizations and follow the standards of practice developed and endorsed by those organizations. They can insist on the same standards of practice from their colleagues, confront those who do not follow standards, and voluntarily subject their own practices to outside review. Fund raisers can also take every opportunity to enlighten nonprofit staff members, board members, donors, volunteers, and the public that professional fund raising is a complex process driven by ethical standards of practice and that the field is primarily made up of honorable, value-driven practitioners.

Fund raisers should be prepared to give philanthropic gifts and to serve as volunteers themselves. Their own philanthropy serves both to provide an example to others and also to meet an expectation others have of them. Fund raisers need to be perceived in their communities as givers.

Implications for Fund-Raising Leaders

Fund-raising leaders include senior practitioners and those in leadership positions in professional organizations. Fund-raising leaders can help fund raisers be more open and honest about the difficulties they face, especially about the tension involved in asking for money. As indicated by the level of discomfort associated with asking for money revealed in this study, open discussion of this issue and training to understand this complex interpersonal transaction are needed. Also needed is more discussion of the changing demographics of donors and volunteers and more acceptance of the need for staff-driven solicitation programs.

Fund-raising leaders must accept responsibility for the continuing sexism and racism in the field. They must support, promote, and undertake the mentoring of women and minorities new to the field and commit to equitable promotions of women and minorities. (Women at all levels of the field must become more knowledgeable about acceptable and competitive salary levels and more skilled in negotiating appropriate salaries for their work.) Without question, fund raisers must accept responsibility for increasing opportunities for minorities in fund raising and for helping them to succeed. Leadership in this effort must come from professional organizations, which must take responsibility for expanding knowledge about the formidable consequences of continued sexism and racism in the field. Professional organizations must also take responsibility for helping fund raisers to develop skills and strategies for promoting women, for retaining men, and for recruiting minorities. If these are not the kinds of professional development opportunities fund raisers now want, the professional development organizations must demonstrate how vital to the field they are.

Professional organizations, which have already made contributions of inestimable value to the field, have significant ongoing responsibilities and multiple opportunities to continue to serve fund raisers, nonprofit organizations, and the public. Leaders of these professional organizations, in their highly visible positions, are role models and must be seen as committed to the field and its progress.

Leaders from several professional organizations have recently worked together to create the Donor Bill of Rights and must continue to collaborate. A united public voice for fund raising and philanthropy is fundamental for the strength and health of the field.

Professional organizations must continue to help practitioners understand and implement ethical standards of practice and treatment of donors. In addition, leadership for many of the initiatives for improving practice recommended by our respondents can only be undertaken by professional organizations. For instance, mentoring programs and networking, two of the key ways respondents believed others can best learn about fund raising, will only thrive if professional organizations, especially at the level of local chapters and affiliates, develop and support them. Professional organizations must provide comprehensive, balanced education and forums for open, nondefensive discussions of the options and issues surrounding certification and licensing for fund raisers.

Professional organizations can play a role in informing practitioners about the value of formal education for fund raising and can work to assure that formal credentials have meaning and will be valued. They can support and promote formal degree programs that include internships, mentorships, and student involvement in professional organization activities. They can lobby for more college-level courses on the nonprofit sector and the history and culture of philanthropy, along with courses on the principles of fund raising. Fund-raising leaders can encourage higher education leaders to include courses on fund raising and philanthropy in existing degree programs in education, social work, health administration, arts administration, environmental administration, ministerial preparation, law, and business.

Professional organizations must also help fund raisers develop the mentoring, managing, and teaching skills that are essential in the informal transfer of knowledge now so prevalent in the field.

Implications for Nonprofit Leaders

Nonprofit leaders include nonprofit executives and board members. Nonprofit leaders must be judicious and thoughtful about compensation practices for fund raisers. They must commit to full disclosure of compensation for fund raisers and all fund-raising costs. They must become articulate, nondefensive proponents of competitive salaries for fund raisers, demonstrating at the same time an understanding of the need to balance market factors against the threat of regulation against salaries that violate public expectations.

Nonprofit leaders must insist on, support, and provide resources for ethical fund raising. They must share responsibility with fund raisers for principled, honorable fund raising. While they must demand cost-effective programs, they must take responsibility for becoming more knowledgeable about the complexities of fund-raising costs and the long-term investments required for long-term fund-raising success. Nonprofit leaders can also take the responsibility for becoming more knowledgeable about fund-raising processes in order to make more enlightened hiring, promotion, retention, and compensation decisions.

Nonprofit organizational practices are critical in correcting gender disparities and in reducing the threat that the fund-raising field could become feminized. Nonprofit leaders must uphold policies to provide equal pay for equal work requiring equal preparation and background. They can create programs for job rotation and internships for women to develop and demonstrate skills in multiple areas, can express commitment to parity in hiring and promoting, and can provide the incentives and disincentives necessary to ensure progress in these activities (Johnsrud and Heck, 1994). In addition, nonprofit leaders can ensure that more women have seats on their boards and build stronger support systems for women, such as flex time and job-sharing programs (Korn/Ferry International, 1993).

Finally, nonprofit leaders have a key responsibility for bringing minorities into fund raising. They can lead their organizations to create incentives for minorities to learn about and become involved in fund raising and create the bridges and incentives to bring minorities into fund raising from other nonprofit areas.

Recommendations for Further Research

The major limitation of this study was the inability to obtain data about fund raisers who are not members of professional organizations. Research on fund raisers who are not members of professional organizations is important in its own right and is critical for assessing the validity of all previous research o fund raisers, including the present study.

One of the original goals of the present research was to learn in detail how fund raisers actually spend their time at work, but we were compelled to eliminate this aspect of the original plan because of time and budget constraints. More information about the day-to-day work that fund raisers do will help increase understanding of fund-raising practice, the variety and meaning of titles for fund raisers, and the progression of responsibilities in fund raising. Important unanswered questions include: What do fund raisers do? How do fund raisers spend their time? How do activities vary by job title, within different types and sizes of nonprofit organizations, or by the dollar amounts of fund-raising goals? In addition to increasing understanding of the body of knowledge underlying the practice of fund raising, this research is critical to the development of standard competencies to define acceptable practices and performance at basic, intermediate, and advanced levels of practice. Perhaps nothing is more critical to the ongoing systematic professional development of the field than this effort.

Also needed is research to define and measure effectiveness in nonprofit organizations of variable types and sizes, to study accountability in fund raising, and to assess the processes by which fund raisers are evaluated and rewarded. Research to describe current practices in evaluation and promotion, as well as to define ideal or preferred practices, would be useful. It would also be useful to learn more about the relationship between effective performance and formal education and other kinds of preparations for work in the field.

Effective performance of fund raisers is dependent upon the fund raiser's knowledge, skills, and values, as well as fit with the organization. Are there different types of fund raisers—different in terms of personality, background, and skills—who are more or less successful in different types of organizations or in certain organizations at different points in their fund-raising histories? Effective performance of fund-raising programs is dependent upon such factors as organizational culture, the nature of the organization's constituents, organizational mission, history of fund-raising efforts, and investment in fund raising. There is a need for continued efforts to define cost-effectiveness in fund-raising programs, taking these multiple variables into account.

Although there is much anecdotal evidence, there is very little empirical information about outsiders' perceptions and expectations of fund raisers. What are the perceptions of fund raisers among the public, nonprofit leaders, volunteers, and donors? What is expected of fund raisers in terms of activity, costs, and results? What are these expectations based on? What values and standards are fund raisers expected to demonstrate?

A number of aspects of the fund-raising field warrant continued monitoring: racial diversity; gender disparity in titles, salaries, and positions; compensation levels and attitudes toward compensation; and job stability. Additionally, it is important to monitor fund raisers' attitudes about themselves and their colleagues and to measure over time potential shifts in educational preparation and attitudes toward the priority for formal education and training related to practice.

Efforts to assess the differences in outcomes of staff-driven and volunteer-driven solicitation efforts would be useful. Decisions regarding choice in this matter often reflect organizational resources and realities rather than adherence to ideal or preferred models of fund-raising practice. Helpful studies would include an assessment of the advantages and disadvantages of both kinds of efforts, as well as the evaluation of bottom-line results and implications for ongoing fund-raising success. Some fund raisers have indicated that as staff-driven programs become more common, the need will increase for even greater long-term organizational commitment on the part of the fund-raising staff, who must take the place of volunteers in long-term relationships with donors. Others have said that visionary fund-raising leaders can modify traditional practice to minimize the negative effects of staff turnover, such as assigning prospects to pairs or teams of fund raisers, instead of individuals, and more sophisticated record-keeping to reduce loss of valuable knowledge and insights about donors when key staff leave. Are there real-life examples of these practices that can be described and analyzed?

Research to describe factors affecting hiring decisions would be helpful. What influences selection decisions? How do nonprofit leaders conceptualize their fund-raising needs and then match these needs with recruitment and selection decisions? What educational and experiential factors are valued?

It would be useful to study fund raisers (their skills and job satisfaction) who were not in the job market but who made job changes after being successfully recruited by other organizations. How often does this occur? What recruitment practices are used? What factors influence fund raisers to leave positions when they were not seeking to make a change? How do these decisions work out for the fund raisers themselves and for the nonprofit organizations recruiting them? What are the characteristics of organizations that offer the best environments for fund raisers?

The practice of fund raising must meet public standards and match public expectations, and there can be no equivocation on these matters. Standards of practice must be carefully defined, information on the costs of fund raising must be carefully developed, and information about the practice and costs of fund raising must be communicated more systematically and more effectively to the public. At the same time, it is necessary for fund raisers to take responsibility for increasing outsiders' understanding of the fund-raising process. Ongoing research in this vital field will promote its continuing professionalization.

References

Angle, H. L., and Perry, J. L. "An Empirical Assessment of Organizational Commitment and Organizational Effectiveness." *Administrative Science Quarterly*, 1981, *26*, 1–14.

Association for Healthcare Philanthropy. *Salary and Benefits Report—U.S.A.* Falls Church, Va.: Association for Healthcare Philanthropy, 1992.

Association for Healthcare Philanthropy. *Salary and Benefits Report—U.S.A.* Falls Church, Va.: Association for Healthcare Philanthropy, 1993.

Bailey, A. L. "Number of Fund Appeals Is Said to Anger Many." *Chronicle of Philanthropy*, Nov. 2, 1993, p. 53.

Barbeito, C. L. "The Non-Profit World Should Apply Its Values to the Salaries It Pays Its Workers." *Chronicle of Philanthropy*, Dec. 11, 1990, pp. 40–41.

Bloland, H. G., and Bornstein, R. "Fund Raising in Transition: Strategies for Professionalization." In D. F. Burlingame and L. J. Hulse (eds.), *Taking Fund Raising Seriously: Advancing the Profession and Practice of Raising Money*. San Francisco: Jossey-Bass, 1991.

Blumenstyk, G. "Colleges Report 4.9 percent Gain in Voluntary Gifts in a Year, But Inflation Adjusted Rate Trails Increase in Costs." *Chronicle of Higher Education*, June 16, 1993, pp. A31–A32.

Bohlen, J. R. *National Society of Fund Raising Executives 1981 Survey Results*. Alexandria, Va.: National Society of Fund Raising Executives, 1981.

Bok, D. *The Cost of Talent: How Executives and Professionals Are Paid and How It Affects America*. New York: Free Press, 1993.

Bremner, R. H. *American Philanthropy*. Chicago: University of Chicago Press, 1988.

Bush, B. H. "The New Reality: Life After Regulation." *Advancing Philanthropy*, Summer 1994, pp. 28–33.

Carbone, R. F. *Fund Raisers of Academe*. College Park, Md.: Clearing House for Research on Fund Raising, 1987.

Carbone, R. F. *Fund Raising as a Profession*. College Park, Md.: Clearing House for Research on Fund Raising, 1989.

"Charities Don't Really Help." Transcript #3875, *Phil Donahue Show*. Dec. 6, 1993. Denver, Colo.: Journal Graphics.

Conry, J. C. "The Feminization of Fund Raising." In D. F. Burlingame and L. J. Hulse, (eds.), *Taking Fund Raising Seriously: Advancing the Profession and Practice of Raising Money.* San Francisco: Jossey-Bass, 1991.

Council on Foundations. *Community Foundations in the United States: 1992 Status.* Washington, D.C.: Council on Foundations, 1994.

Dale, H. P. "Tax-Exempt Organizations: Winds of Change." Norman A. Sugarman Memorial Lecture, Mandel Center for Nonprofit Organizations, Case Western Reserve University, Cleveland, Ohio, Mar. 20, 1991.

Dundjerski, M. "United Way: 1 percent Increase in Gifts." *Chronicle of Philanthropy,* Sept. 7, 1995, p. 27.

Duronio, M. A., and Loessin, B. A. *Effective Fund Raising in Higher Education: Ten Success Stories.* San Francisco: Jossey-Bass, 1991.

Eisenberg, P. "Press Coverage Sends a Message to Non-Profits: Clean Up Your Act." *Chronicle of Philanthropy,* July 13, 1993, pp. 41–43.

Eisenberger, R., and Huntington, R. "Perceived Organizational Support." *Journal of Applied Psychology,* 1986, *71*(3), 500–507.

Eisenberger, R., Fasolo, P., and Davis-LaMastro, V. "Perceived Organizational Support and Employee Diligence, Commitment, and Innovation." *Journal of Applied Psychology,* 1990, *75*(1), 51–59.

Farrell, D., and Rusbult, C. E. "Exchange Variables as Predictors of Job Satisfaction, Job Commitment, and Turnover: The Impact of Rewards, Costs, Alternatives, and Investments." *Organizational Behavior and Human Performance,* 1981, *27*, 78–95.

"Fund Raising's Recovery." *Chronicle of Philanthropy,* Apr. 19, 1994, pp. 1, 22–24.

Funiciello, T. *Tyranny of Kindness: Dismantling the Welfare System to End Poverty in America.* New York: Atlantic Monthly Press, 1993.

"Gallup Poll: Most Favor More Oversight of Charities." *NonProfit Times,* Oct. 1993, p. 6.

Gaul, G. M., and Borowski, N. A. "Nonprofits: America's Growth Industry." *Philadelphia Inquirer,* Apr. 18, 1993, pp. A1–A10.

Gaul, G. M., and Borowski, N. A. "The Rise of Medical Empires." *Philadelphia Inquirer,* Apr. 19, 1993, pp. A1–A12.

Gaul, G. M., and Borowski, N. A. "A Tax Break Colleges Can Bank On." *Philadelphia Inquirer,* Apr. 20, 1993, pp. A1–A10.

Gaul, G. M., and Borowski, N. A. "The IRS, An Enforcer That Can't Keep Up." *Philadelphia Inquirer,* Apr. 21, 1993, pp. A1–A10.

Gaul, G. M., and Borowski, N. A. "In High-Level Jobs at Nonprofits, Charity Really Pays." *Philadelphia Inquirer,* Apr. 22, 1993, pp. A1–A18.

Gaul, G. M., and Borowski, N. A. "For Nonprofits Only: A Cheap Pool of Money." *Philadelphia Inquirer,* Apr. 23, 1993, pp. A1–A26.

Gaul, G. M., and Borowski, N. A. "Foundations Build a Giant Nest Egg." *Philadelphia Inquirer,* Apr. 24, 1993, pp. A1–A6.

Glick, N. L. "Job Satisfaction Among Academic Administrators." *Research in Higher Education,* 1992, *33*(5), 625–639.

Goldstein, H. "The Fortunate 500: Paying High Salaries to Non-Profit CEOs Is Not Immoral." *Chronicle of Philanthropy,* June 1, 1993, pp. 37–38.

Goss, K. A. "Why Do Rich People Give to Charity?" *Chronicle of Philanthropy,* Mar. 8, 1994, pp. 1, 13, 15–16.

Goss, K. A., and Moore, J. "More Scrutiny for Charity Salaries." *Chronicle of Philanthropy,* May 17, 1994, pp. 1, 29–36.

Gouldner, A. W. "Cosmopolitans and Locals: Toward an Analysis of Latent Social Roles—I." *Administrative Science Quarterly,* 1957a, 2, 281–306.

Gouldner, A. W. "Cosmopolitans and Locals: Toward an Analysis of Latent Social Roles—II." *Administrative Science Quarterly,* 1957b, 2, 444–480.

Gray, S., and Greene, E. "Big Salaries Just Keep Going Up." *Chronicle of Philanthropy,* Sept. 7, 1995, pp. 1, 33–34.

Greene, E., Greene, S. G., and Moore, J. "A Generation Prepares to Transfer Its Trillions." *Chronicle of Philanthropy,* Nov. 16, 1993, pp. 1, 8, 11–12.

Greene, S. G. "The Non-Profit World: A Statistical Portrait." *Chronicle of Philanthropy,* Jan. 28, 1992a, p. 24.

Greene, S. G. "Compliance with Salary Rules: Often Grudging." *Chronicle of Philanthropy,* Mar. 24, 1992b, pp. 27–28, 33.

Greene, S. G., and Moore, J. "Interest Still High in Charity Salaries." *Chronicle of Philanthropy,* Apr. 6, 1993, pp. 1, 30–33.

Harrah-Conforth, J., and Borsos, J. "The Evolution of Professional Fund Raising: 1890–1990." In D. F. Burlingame and L. J. Hulse (eds.), *Taking Fund Raising Seriously: Advancing the Profession and Practice of Raising Money.* San Francisco: Jossey-Bass, 1991.

Hodgkinson, V. A., and Weitzman, M. A. *Giving and Volunteering in the United States: Findings From a National Survey.* Washington, D.C.: Independent Sector, 1992.

Hopkins, B. R. *The Law of Fund-Raising.* (2nd ed.) New York: Wiley, 1996.

Independent Sector. *Ethics and the Nation's Voluntary and Philanthropic Community: Obedience to the Unenforceable.* Washington, D.C.: Independent Sector, 1991.

Independent Sector. *Summary of Philadelphia Inquirer Articles.* Unpublished paper. Washington, D.C.: Independent Sector, 1993.

Internal Revenue Service. *Statistics of Income Bulletin,* Spring 1987, *6*(4).

Johnsrud, L. K., and Heck, R. H. "Administrative Promotion Within a University: The Cumulative Impact of Gender." *Journal of Higher Education*, 1994, *65*(1), 23–44.

Kaplan, A. E. (ed.). *Giving USA: The Annual Report on Philanthropy for the Year 1993.* New York: AAFRC Trust for Philanthropy, 1994.

Kaplan, A. E. (ed.). *Giving USA: The Annual Report on Philanthropy for the Year 1994.* New York: AAFRC Trust for Philanthropy, 1995.

Kelly, K. S. *Fund Raising and Public Relations: A Critical Analysis.* Hillsdale, N.J.: Erlbaum, 1991.

Kelly, K. S. *Building Fund-Raising Theory: An Empirical Test of Four Models of Practice.* Essays on Philanthropy, no. 12. Indianapolis: Indiana University Center on Philanthropy, 1994.

Korn/Ferry International. *Decade of the Executive Woman.* New York: Korn/Ferry International, 1993.

Leatherman, C. "What's Fair Compensation for a University Chief? Opinions Differ." *Chronicle of Higher Education*, May 5, 1993, pp. A13, A16.

Lewis, P. "President's Message." *NSFRE News*, Mar. 1995, p. 1.

Lichtenberg, N. *American Foundations Oral History Project Final Report.* Bloomington: Indiana University Oral History Research Center, 1993.

Lodahl, T. M., and Kejner, M. "The Definition and Measurement of Job Involvement." *Journal of Applied Psychology*, 1965, *49*(1), 24–33.

McIver, L. "Salaries Are Flat at Nonprofits, But Fringes Are Hot, Hot, Hot." *NonProfit Times*, Feb. 1996, pp. 23–27.

McNamee, M. "The Feminization of CASE." *Currents*, Sept. 1990a, pp. 8–12.

McNamee, M. "The Outlook for Women." *Currents*, Sept. 1990b, pp. 13–14.

McNamee, M. "The Salary Surge." *Currents*, Sept. 1990c, pp. 15–21.

Meyer, J. P., and others. "Organizational Commitment and Job Performance: It's the Nature of the Commitment That Counts." *Journal of Applied Psychology*, 1989, *74*(1), 152–156.

Millar, B. "United Way Stops Aramony's Pay, Fires Chief Financial Officer." *Chronicle of Philanthropy*, Mar. 24, 1992, pp. 34–35.

Millar, B., and Moore, J. "Salary Raises for Non-Profit CEO's Are Found to Outpace Inflation." *Chronicle of Philanthropy*, Sept. 6, 1994, pp. 38–39.

Mongon, G. J., Jr. *NSFRE Profile 1985 Membership Career Survey.* Alexandria, Va.: National Society of Fund Raising Executives, 1985.

Mongon, G. J., Jr. "Profile 1988 NSFRE Membership Career Survey." *NSFRE Journal*, Winter 1988, pp. 20–42.

Mongon, G. J., Jr. *NSFRE Profile: 1992 Membership Survey.* Alexandria, Va.: National Society of Fund Raising Executives, 1992.

Mongon, G. J., Jr. *NSFRE Profile: 1995 Membership Survey. Preliminary Report.* Alexandria, Va.: National Society of Fund Raising Executives, 1995.

Mooney, C. L. "Study Examines Turnover Rates in 12 Campus Jobs." *Chronicle of Higher Education,* Feb. 10, 1993, p. A16.

Moore, J. "Two Years Later, A Scandal's Legacy." *Chronicle of Philanthropy,* May 17, 1994, pp. 28–29.

Morris, J. H., and Steers, R. M. "Structural Influences on Organizational Commitment." *Journal of Vocational Behavior,* 1980, *17,* 50–57.

Mowday, R., Porter, L., and Steers, R. M. *Employee-Organization Linkages: The Psychology of Commitment, Absenteeism, and Turnover.* New York: Academic Press, 1982.

National Society of Fund Raising Executives. *Guidelines to the Standards of Professional Practice.* Alexandria, Va.: National Society of Fund Raising Executives, 1995.

Nielsen, W. A. "Will the Leaders of the Non-Profit World Heed Bill Clinton's Call for Sacrifice?" *Chronicle of Philanthropy,* Feb. 23, 1993, pp. 57–58.

Odendahl, T., and Fischer, M. *Gender and the Professionalization of Philanthropy.* Essays on Philanthropy, no. 19. Indianapolis: Indiana University Center on Philanthropy, 1996.

Panas, J. *Born to Raise: What Makes a Great Fundraiser? What Makes a Fundraiser Great?* Chicago: Pluribus Press, 1988.

Pomeranz, R. C. "Let's Run Charities Like the Big Businesses They Are." *Chronicle of Philanthropy,* Apr. 5, 1994, p. 44.

Porter, L., Steers, R., and Mowday, R. "Organizational Commitment, Job Status, and Turnover Among Psychiatric Technicians." *Journal of Applied Psychology,* 1974, *59,* 603–609.

Preston, A. "Compensation Patterns in the Sector." In L. Cohen and D. R. Young (eds.), *Careers for Doers and Dreamers: A Guide to Management Careers in the Nonprofit Sector.* New York: Foundation Center, 1989.

Renz, L., Lawrence, S., and Treiber, R. R. *Foundation Giving: Yearbook of Facts and Figures on Private, Corporate, and Community Foundations.* New York: Foundation Center, 1995.

Rocque, A. "Non-Profit Executives Get 6.4 percent Increase in Pay." *Chronicle of Philanthropy,* Oct. 4, 1994, p. 45.

Rosso, H. A., and Associates. *Achieving Excellence in Fund Raising: A Comprehensive Guide to Principles, Strategies, and Methods.* San Francisco: Jossey-Bass, 1991.

Seiler, T., and Tempel, E. R. "Trustees and Staff: Building Effective Fundraising Teams." In K. Grace and T. Seiler (eds.), *Achieving Trustee Involvement in Fundraising.* New Directions for Philanthropic Fundraising, no. 4. San Francisco: Jossey-Bass, 1994.

Sheldon, M. E. "Investments and Involvements as Mechanisms Producing Commitment to the Organization." *Administrative Science Quarterly,* 1971, *16,* 143–150.

Special Libraries Association. *SLA Biennial Salary Survey 1995.* Washington, D.C.: Special Libraries Association, 1995.

Steers, R. M. "Antecedents and Outcomes of Organizational Commitment." *Administrative Science Quarterly,* 1977, *22,* 46–56.

Steers, R. M., and Porter, L. W. *Motivation and Work Behavior.* (2nd ed.) New York: McGraw-Hill, 1979.

Stevens, J. N., Beyer, J. N., and Trice, H. M. "Assessing Personal, Role, and Organizational Predictors of Managerial Commitment." *Academy of Management Journal,* 1978, *21*(3), 380–396.

Thomas, E. G. "Flight Records." *Currents,* Oct. 1987, pp. 6–11.

Turk, J. V. "The Changing Face of CASE." *Currents,* June 1986a, pp. 8–13.

Turk, J. V. "The Shifting Salary Scene." *Currents,* June 1986b, 15–20.

Van Til, J. "The Nonprofit Salary Gap." *NonProfit Times,* Oct. 1993, p. 14.

Wiener, Y., and Gechman, A. S. "Commitment: A Behavioral Approach to Job Involvement." *Journal of Vocational Behavior,* 1977, *10,* 47–52.

Williams, G. "Still Getting a Direct Response." *Chronicle of Philanthropy,* Sept. 7, 1993, pp. 29, 34–35, 38.

Williams, R. L. "Survey on Advancement." *Currents,* Feb. 1996, pp. 8–22.

Worth, M. J., and Asp, J. W., II. *The Development Officer in Higher Education: Toward an Understanding of the Role.* ASHE-ERIC Higher Education Report, no. 4. Washington, D.C.: George Washington University, Graduate School of Education and Human Development, 1994.

Young, D. *If Not For Profit, For What? A Behavioral Theory of the Nonprofit Sector Based on Entrepreneurship.* San Francisco: New Lexington Press, 1983.

Index